Ari Livne

# TIN SOLDIER IN A CARDBOARD BOX

## A Young Boy in Hiding: Austria–Belgium–France

Ari Livne

# TIN SOLDIER IN A CARDBOARD BOX

A Young Boy in Hiding:
Austria–Belgium–France

Translated from the Hebrew by Ora Cummings

Yad Vashem ★ Jerusalem
The International Institute for Holocaust Research

Ari Livne
*Chayal Bdil Bekufsat Karton*

*Academic Editor*: Jeannine (Levana) Frenk
*Language and Production Editor*: Gayle Green

© 2015 All rights to the English edition are reserved to Yad Vashem
P.O.B. 3477, Jerusalem 9103401, Israel
publications.marketing@yadvashem.org.il
First published in Hebrew by Gvanim Publishers, 2010

ISBN 978-965-308-490-2

Typesetting: PageUp
Printed in Israel by Art Plus — Green Printing, Jerusalem

*In memory of my parents,*
*Sara and Elias Lipa,*
*Uncle Salo and Aunt Hanna'le Stern.*

*To my wife, Yehudith, and my children,*
*Noah and Assaf, and their families.*

*With love.*

# CONTENTS

# CHAPTER ONE

# *NATHANIEL*

“**B**etween 1943 and 1945, I was given the name Dieudonné, which means 'God gave.' The equivalent name in Hebrew is Nathaniel.”

*It is freezing cold. From a distance I can see high, snow-covered mountains, their peaks as sharp as swords. Nature reveals itself to me in all its glory. The landscape is familiar, although I have never been in this place before.*

*All around me unidentified figures are moving weightlessly, like ghosts. They are floating above the ridge. I am watching intently. I am lying in a trench near the railway lines and next to me are many people I know. Suddenly, familiar faces are replaced by ones I have never seen before, but it is obvious to me that they are all part of my gang.*

*The figures are darting about, disappearing in a flash before reappearing. I make a superhuman effort to focus my thoughts, but have no success. Still struggling against the invisible powers of nature, I am trying to get a grip on some kind of image in order to release myself from the paralysis from which I am suffering. One figure disappears for a second and now, here it is back again, standing to attention as if obeying an order. This figure is someone I know very well.*

*We are waiting for a train full of Jewish children on its way to some obscure destination. We are here to sabotage the railway lines, armed with guns to cover the children as they escape. The figure beside me is that of the commander. His name resonates forcefully; everyone is shouting "Nathaniel." From out of the dense darkness the train materializes, my head spins. There is a gigantic explosion; children are running in every direction, I fall into a black hole. Then, all around, there is silence, and from my throat a silent, suffocating cry emerges.*

I awoke with a shout, my body was covered with sweat and I was shaking all over. I opened my eyes and suddenly noticed Aunt Angele leaning over me and stroking my damp hair in an attempt to reassure me. Her face was full of concern. Confused, trapped in my dream, I was unable to understand what was happening around me. Aunt Angele explained that I had called out in my dream, repeating the name "Nathaniel, Nathaniel" several times, and as she mouthed the name, the dream suddenly came back to me.

That wasn't the first time. Lately, I've been dreaming a lot about that figure who visits me in my dreams and causes me indescribable agitation. He takes on the image of a knight, shrouded in the splendor of a bygone age, but still very close and familiar. The knight of my dreams is a Jew, strong and heroic. He punishes the German murderers who are harming us Jews, insulting and humiliating us, ridiculing and beating us, laughing at us hysterically and, finally, killing us.

The Nathaniel who appears in my dreams is a figure of bravery and fearlessness, a bold and courageous fighter defending his nation. Admittedly, I am only eight years old, but I yearn to fight by his side. However, I don't always manage to appear in my own dreams and this makes me sad.

I remember well the stories and fables told to me by the white-bearded rabbi my parents contracted to teach me Bible stories. He used to come to our home in Brussels when I was still in hiding with my parents. Sometimes, my father would join our lessons and vigilantly follow my responses, replies and comments; and if I sometimes appeared to be losing my train of thought, he would intervene immediately and force me to repeat what we had just learned, all the while expanding the question and delving into the analysis, often in what seemed to me to be an exaggerated manner. He seemed to have forgotten that he was dealing with a boy of six or seven years old. Sometimes, before I fell asleep, I would conjure up images of certain characters whom I'd met in the Bible stories and feel close to them. These thoughts helped me to escape the sights of suffering and humiliation that were taking place beyond the walls of our home. After a while, my parents asked the rabbi to stop visiting us because they feared that his visits might put us at risk.

Often, after witnessing one of these painful incidents, I would be overcome by a colossal rage. When my father noticed this and thinking I might do something stupid that would cost us dearly, he would lay his hand on my shoulder and pull me towards him. Being aware of my turbulent nature, my parents were very strict about my behavior, especially when we went outside. They would signal to me with a finger not to utter a sound and we would then make a hasty retreat. We tried hard not to attract attention; we lowered our eyes and did everything we could to hide the yellow star[1] that was fastened to our clothing with a safety pin. We tried to blend into our surroundings, to be as inconspicuous as possible.

I remember one particular incident from this period that has embedded itself deep in my soul. On one of the occasions when we stayed in Brussels, our attention was attracted by a large pickup truck that was parked by the sidewalk. Three German soldiers were sitting in the back of the truck. A car with police or government number plates was parked alongside the truck. Both vehicles were parked a short distance from where we were living at the time, on a long and beautiful boulevard that cut the road into two parts. The whole length of the boulevard was lined with tall trees, at the base of which there were handsome benches made of decorative wrought iron. In

---

1    In Belgium, the Germans imposed the wearing of the yellow star at the beginning of June 1942.

the afternoon hours, when the weather permitted, the benches were usually occupied by elderly people.

It was already quite late in the day and darkness was falling. As we passed the parked vehicles, we noticed a man and a woman coming out of a nearby house, followed by two small children; the four were being pushed along roughly by a couple of people in uniform. The uniform was not that of the German Army, it was dark blue or black, possibly belonging to the Belgium police.[2] Unlike the German soldiers, they carried no rifles but they had pistols, which they kept in holsters attached to their belts.

The soldiers sitting in the truck did not react to the event, as if it had nothing to do with them. The two in the dark uniforms continued to push the terrified family into the car. The father of the family tried to protest and to talk to the two men, but they just shouted at him, in French, I think, and continued to push them aggressively, making incoherent threats. My parents and I were walking down the boulevard at the time, only a few meters away from the place of the incident. My father, who was a few steps behind me, ran forward suddenly and placed his hand on my shoulder with considerable deliberation. He must have noticed from my stance that I was about to jump forward and attack the uniformed men. I was naïve enough to believe that I had the power to save that family.

After this and other similar incidents, my father would sit with me and give me lengthy explanations of what was permitted and what was forbidden and in this way he taught me how to take care of myself. He also explained to me that the foolish act that I had been about to commit could have been extremely costly not only to me but also to those close to me. He went over this repeatedly until he was sure that I had it all thoroughly internalized. This lesson of self-control and restraint was of great significance. Later on, during the war, when I was forced to cope with similar situations on my own, there were countless opportunities for me to put my father's doctrine into practice.

---

2   In arresting Jews, the Germans used Belgian auxiliary forces established from among the local fascist movements. They belonged to paramilitary organizations and had their own uniforms.

Whenever my parents and I left the house we were obliged to wear the yellow star. My mother would be the first to step outside, I would leave a minute later and after another minute it would be my father's turn to leave. We were careful to maintain eye contact with each other. To be accurate, my father and I oversaw my mother; we were not allowed to lose sight of her. My father walked behind me and he watched over my mother and me. We practiced this movement of ours several times and everything went all right.

My parents explained to me that this system decreased the chances of being captured all together. The instructions I received were that in the event of one of us being arrested, it would be each one for himself. We also practiced and even role-played the appropriate behavior for different situations. In theory, I was prepared to cope with all kinds of unexpected situations, but it was relatively easy for me, since I knew that my father would come to my rescue whenever necessary. This sense of security gave me a lot of strength.

Every few months, we would change the apartment in which we were living and hiding, in order to evade the German soldiers who were constantly attempting to capture Jews, wherever they were. I might be exaggerating slightly when I refer to them as apartments; we mostly occupied isolated, single rooms, which always had a separate entrance. As far as I remember, those rooms were located on the top floor of the buildings or in the attic. There was always a large bed in the middle of the room for my parents and a small bed for me. Usually, there was also a table, a few chairs and a closet. The walls were covered in faded chintzy wallpaper. I remember asking myself why there wasn't a single picture on any of the walls, but could find no answer. In spite of the miserable appearance of these rooms, my parents always made a point of referring to them as "home." Thus, we would always be "going home" or "leaving home." All this talk about home gave a semblance of warmth to our room and may even have helped us, with a little imagination, to "feel at home."

My parents were cultured people; they loved to attend operas and concerts. In her youth, my mother had played the piano. People who knew her from then said she had been very talented. Perhaps she had had dreams of becoming a famous concert pianist, but the circumstances of her life put an end to her fantasies. Still, in spite of the tense situation they were living in, my parents would still go to the opera or to a concert, leaving me with two people I was especially fond of — Uncle Salo and his wife, Hanna'le. Uncle Salo was my mother's brother and he and Hanna'le had not been married for long. Hanna'le was very beautiful and exotic-looking. She laughed a lot and managed to infect everyone around her with her constant good spirits. She was filled with the joys of life and had an endless sense of optimism. A very strong and intimate relationship developed between the three of us, especially since they were the only people with whom I could, or to be more accurate, with whom I was allowed to talk.

My parents, Elias and Sara, on their wedding day.
Vienna, December 1933.

A unique relationship developed between my parents and me, since we spent most of our time together. Sometimes I would skip school[3] and spend entire days in their company, in our single room. The mutual danger that was constantly hanging over our heads tightened our relationship and made us even closer. There was a feeling of impermanence, a sense that the situation was about to change, and I held onto the relationship with my parents, uncle and aunt with all my might. I was aware of the fact that this family framework was completely temporary and it would not be long before it collapsed. This feeling was very tangible and took control of me to such an extent that I suffered great anxiety, especially at night. I wanted to stop time, but I felt it slipping through my fingers.

In the tough world in which we were living, my parents and I managed to build for ourselves an island of happiness, but it was a fragile island surrounded by a sea of violence and we tried to gulp down the moments of happiness. I remember my mother telling me about the famous Roman poet, Quintus Horatius Flaccus, widely known as Horace, who coined the Latin phrase *Carpe Diem* (seize the day), and she went on to explain to me the meaning of his poem: Life is short, moments of happiness are rare and every good minute must be experienced and enjoyed to the full. There was a discrepancy between the desire to seize the moments of happiness and warmth, not to allow them to slip away, and the terrible slowness in which time went by. Sometimes, it seemed as if time stood still.

Since the single room in which we lived had no space for more than two beds, a closet and a small table, it was impossible to move about and play. I remember lying on my bed most of the time and playing with the only toys I possessed in those years, a tin soldier and a small box made of some kind of corrugated material, possibly cardboard, both painted green. The box served as barracks, a bed for

3    From December 1941, Jewish children were forbidden to attend Belgian schools. In order to establish separate schools for Jewish children the Germans enlisted the Association of Jews in Belgium — the equivalent of the Jewish Council and the only Jewish organization recognized by the German authorities.

the soldier, a house and a training facility and I played with those two articles for hours, for entire days.

I created all kinds of connections between the soldier and the box. That box — a nondescript object with no specific purpose — stimulated my imagination. Every day, it played a different role and I was never bored with it or disappointed by it. As for the soldier, it was only ever a soldier. I couldn't imagine it as a baby that I was placing in a crib or a boy hiding in a shelter as a bomb attack was taking place. It was impossible to imagine the soldier as a mother washing herself in the sink or as a father standing and praying. The box filled all the roles I could conjure up for it, but the soldier was never more than just a soldier. Sometimes, I would struggle with the soldier for days in an attempt to give him another image, another role, but I was always unsuccessful. This often anguished me and I discussed it with my mother. She explained that the best playthings, the kind that get your imagination moving, are usually mundane, inanimate, day-to-day objects that can be found everywhere and were not necessarily real toys. She used to say, "Take a shoe and a sock, take a pencil and an eraser, take a toothbrush, take anything in your vicinity and your imagination will do the rest." But, again, I was up against a technical issue — there weren't enough things or objects in my vicinity. We were living in a room with three or four suitcases and their contents were quite meager; they were mostly my parents' clothes that I wasn't allowed to touch in case I damaged them or got them dirty. So, I had no choice but to go back to the soldier and the box. They were mine and I could play with them to my heart's content.

But, at some stage, I decided to stop playing with the tin soldier and box. I made do with just my imagination, without having to hold anything in my hands. Everything now took place inside my head and I spent long hours in bed, daydreaming. I imagined myself playing with toys — a different toy every time — and I really enjoyed it. Once, I was riding a bicycle over isolated paths in a virgin forest, surrounded by tall shady trees, with a burning sun penetrating through the branches and leaves; and on another occasion, I was riding a horse across a beach with giant waves spraying me with salty water. I played in a big room with other boys and girls and we laughed and squabbled alternately as our mothers stood nearby and gave us the occasional smile.

I noticed after a while that my mother was worried. She asked me why I was no longer playing with my two toys. I explained what had been happening in my mind recently and I remember that she couldn't reconcile herself to the new situation. I even remember my parents talking quietly in the evening and throwing glances towards me, glances that were full of distress and sadness. Often, I noticed tears pouring from Mother's eyes when she looked at me. I pretended not to see anything, although I was aware of the situation.

Every day or so, Mother, Father and I would set out in our usual order to shop for food. We never returned with full bags, only with a few vegetables, some fruit and various other commodities. There didn't seem to be much of a choice. Maybe the prices were too high.[4] All we wanted in those troubled times was to attract as little attention as possible. My mother cooked our food in a corner of the room, doing her best to extract the utmost, or even more, out of each of the ingredients. We ate a lot of turnips in those days, as well as potatoes; sometimes there would be a little meat, peas and beans and, for dessert, there would be some sweetish cooked rhubarb. The ingredients were always the same, but my mother managed to compose a varied menu out of them that would have pleased any gourmand. Afterwards, we would lick our fingers!

I believe that the warm nest we managed to build for ourselves and all the love my mother put into her cooking, which was stamped with special flavors and aromas have, ever since, been carved deep in my memory. The room would be filled with the aromas of a feast, of a holiday. From time to time, Mother would bake a cake, according to the Viennese style of baking. Sometimes, this would be a many-layered cake, perhaps with a chocolate cream filling. Each of us was served a long, slender slice like an autumn leaf. We would make the cake last for about two weeks.

---

4    In wartime Belgium, food was purchased with food coupons, which were not available to illegal residents. Clearly the author's parents used their own resources to buy food.

Mother did not make do only with cooking delicious dishes. She invested a great deal of effort in the presentation of her food. We didn't have a set of handsome dishes or tablecloths, we had no special accessories or fabulous decorations; all our belongings consisted of what could be packed into two or three suitcases — a few items that my parents took with them when they fled. But we had three plates decorated with tiny flowers and farmyard pictures, in the Austrian style, depicting country girls against a background of a church and red-roofed houses, and we owned three aristocratic-looking, long-stemmed crystal wine glasses, which, of course, we used for drinking water. Our silver cutlery, too, was decorated with images of country children. It was all rather heavy and elaborate, in the style of the Austrian bourgeoisie. Sometimes the room we lived in had a relatively large dining table, round or oblong. But in most of the rooms, there was only a small round, three-legged table like the ones in Parisian cafes, which were meant for a single diner. At every meal, as she had done in our home in Vienna, Mother would spread over the table a white tablecloth with small flowers embroidered around its edges. I don't remember any other tablecloth and I assume that Mother laundered it often as it always looked starched and new. These objects imparted to the laid table a festive look, *gemütlich*, as Mother said in German. The sight of that table filled us with joy and, for a few moments, we felt a spiritual lift. Conversation around the table was usually lively, focusing on pleasant events and we would feel as if we were participating in a celebratory feast in another world. Those moments were magical and highly charged. We did all we could to keep our emotions under control.

At those times and throughout that period, my father tried to instill in me a Jewish education. He did this in his own special way — tenderly, sensitively and intensely, as if entrusting me with a rare treasure, a secret code that I was to protect all my life, and it would be he who would show me the way. Since the rabbi had already stopped visiting our home, Father undertook to fill the void.

He was a good storyteller and every evening he would tell me about one or another biblical character. His descriptions were very colorful, very human and at the same time, they were heroic and surrounded by a special aura; figures who had turned into heroes and whom I enjoyed being associated with. He often repeated the story of David, the clever young boy, who was skilled in battle and fought and defeated the giant Goliath, later becoming King of Israel. Sometimes, he would try to teach me some lesson and would say in simple words, enlisting all the mental powers and optimism he saved for me, "You'll see, the small and persecuted Jewish nation will ultimately defeat the Nazi monster, in spite of its power." And he would add, "Understand, the Jews were once a nation of fighters who fought against the Romans, who were no less strong than the Germans today. Our nation rose up courageously against the biggest empire in history, which was unable to bend us." And he said, staring deep into my eyes, "Don't ever forget that we are a nation of obstinate fighters. We must not be judged only by what is happening now." I looked into his eyes and saw a profound sadness. I wondered what exactly my father wanted of me. What did he expect from me? Still, his words sunk deep, deep inside me. As for my mother, she used to light candles on the Sabbath eve and, by doing so, she turned the festive meal into a memory I could keep with me always.

Years later, I understood my Father's behavior and I realized that he was trying to help me overcome my doubts, to reinstate my faith in my ability to survive and, especially, my lost pride. Everything they did wrapped my father's words with an additional casing of vivid memories.

We usually avoided all communication with the other tenants in the buildings we lived in, but we made an exception in one case. This happened when we moved into an attic apartment belonging to a Belgian Christian family — a couple and their seventeen- or eighteen-year-old son — who also lived in the building. The boy played football, apparently for a good club, because he owned some handsome sports clothes like those of professional footballers — a white shirt with dark stripes, black shorts, thick white socks that almost reached up to his knees, a pair of shin pads that he pushed into his socks and some football boots that aroused my envy. All of these items were placed inside a large black sports bag. The couple and their son were pleasant, friendly people and their sympathy for the lifestyle we were forced to live was genuine. They even invited us a few times to eat with them, despite the personal risk involved, and we were extremely grateful for such gestures.

Sometimes, the landlady would come up to our room with some sweet pastries or some other delicious dish she had cooked. Mother felt uncomfortable for being unable to reciprocate. Still, we were convinced that the landlady was acting out of genuine generosity and pity for a family that was being persecuted for having committed no crime. My mother must have understood that it was impossible to refuse and continued to accept all the good things we were fortunate enough to receive. She realized that any refusal would be construed as a painful insult to the kind lady, who probably saw her acts as a religious undertaking of the first order. The landlady was very humane and attentive and her husband, who was always very helpful, was obviously concerned as well. We felt excellent in their company and trusted them, but after a stay of two or three months, we had to leave, probably because we had become overexposed in that apartment.

I was very sad the day before we left because I had become quite friendly with the football player. It was one of the few times I had ever had a friend, despite the age difference between us. He was a pleasant, smiling lad and I think he was fond of me, too. Once, he even allowed me to delve into his holy of holies, his football bag, which had in it all the kit necessary for a serious player. Whenever he returned from a game, his mother would wash, iron and fold everything and then return it all to the black bag. The bag emitted an unforgettable smell of cleanliness and health. I wanted to accompany him to the football pitch, but, of course, I didn't get permission.

Sometimes, my parents would allow me to go with him down to the yard behind the house to play football. He had a real football and I kicked it hard and enthusiastically. My friend would sometimes dribble with the ball and try to teach me a few moves. Since he was tall and well built, I asked him to teach me some boxing and he taught me how to defend and also to attack. We punched each other but he never hurt me. Those lessons in that dark and dingy backyard were to be quite helpful later in my life, after I'd been separated from my parents.

Shortly after my parents and I had left that building and moved to a new place, my mother came home one day looking very agitated. Mother told us that the home of those good people had been hit during the last bomb attack. The parents of the footballer had been killed. Their son had been in the outside privy at exactly that moment and was saved. My parents went over to the site of the tragedy but refused to take me along. When they returned home, they appeared horrified and preferred not to discuss what they had seen. We never again saw the son, who had been such a good friend to me. I mourned for them together with my parents, but I wanted to see the son again and I behaved badly for a few days. My obstinacy weighed on my parents but they didn't reproach me; instead, they helped me overcome my pain with soft words and much patience.

*  *  *

For me, it all began in 1938, with the annexation of Austria to Germany — the Anschluss — and my parents' decision to leave Vienna.[5] Most of my mother's family lived in Vienna, with the exception of her oldest brother, who had immigrated to the Land of Israel in the 1920s. In 1938, my family, still in Vienna, consisted of my grandmother who had been widowed many years earlier, my parents and my mother's three brothers and their wives. A few months after Austria was annexed to Germany, they all left and made their way to Belgium. My grandmother was the only one who made it to Israel, where she joined her eldest son.

My memories of Vienna remain dim and hazy. Apart from a few blurred photographs of my room and the red toy car I had there, I remember nothing. But, what I do have carved in my memory is the yearning for my life in Vienna. I remember it as a soft and protected world; a world that turned in an instant into a hostile and treacherous one.

---

5   The Anschluss ("connection" or "unity") was the occupation and annexation of Austria into Nazi Germany in 1938, which ended Austria's independence as a republic. It was followed by a wave of emigration, consisting of Jews and members of left-wing organizations and parties. A few thousand Jews fled to Belgium and France in order to avoid Nazi persecution.

The journey from Austria to Belgium was hard and dangerous. The route we took was complex and roundabout and everything we did was illegal. I was three-and-a-half at the time, so my memories of the journey are blurred and fractured. But, there are moments when the memories take the form of brief, but especially clear, flashes. I remember well the long hikes, when I wept from sheer exhaustion and was carried for hours on my father's shoulders even though he had to help my mother, too. For some of the time, we walked in full daylight, while other parts of the journey had to be made under the cover of darkness, to avoid being detected. When we decided to stop for a break or for the night, we would locate some hidden spot in the forest and rest on the ground or on the tree stumps, which were scattered all around. I don't know if my father was able to sleep at all because every time I awoke I found him up and alert.

Police arrested us one day and I remember the three of us in a small prison cell. I also recall being thirsty and my father banging on a door and shouting, "Water for the child," and someone actually bringing me some water. Our journey from Austria, of which only a few events remain carved in my memory, culminated in the Belgian city of Antwerp.

Our first encounter with the Belgian authorities is described in documents drafted by the local gendarmerie on September 26, 1938 shortly after we had arrived in the Belgian town of Eupen,[6] near the German border, not far from the city of Aachen. I obtained the document in December 2007 and the following is a translation of the original French:

> (…) *These foreigners arrived in Aachen by train, of their own volition. At the railway station in Aachen, they met a man by the name of Marcus and crossed the border in the same way as he had done. They claimed that they had at their disposal money that is in the possession of a family member named Bergstein, who lives in Antwerp and that it is their desire to go to his home, where they will wait until their departure to South America.*

---

6   Eupen was annexed by Germany during the Nazi occupation of Belgium.

*Since these foreigners did not possess a passport with an entry permit to Belgium, signed by a Belgian consular representative or a Belgian diplomat, we deported them in accordance with the rules.*

*Hubert Jerusalem provided the following declaration on September 17, 1938: Yesterday at about 15:30 in the afternoon I was taking a walk in the woods across the River Getzbach, when I encountered three men, a woman and a boy. I talked to them and they told me about their problems. When I understood that they didn't know where to go, I offered to lead them to Eupen. I helped them cross the Getzbach and led them through the woods to the place known as "Hundswagen." The walk took a long time because they were exhausted, especially the woman, and they had to make frequent stops to rest. When we had almost reached the new road leading to the dam I suddenly heard a car accelerating. I ran to see who was driving and at the same moment you noticed me. I am not connected to any organization that secretly brings Jews across to Eupen and I have received no money for doing so. I acted as I did purely out of humanitarian motives. (…)*

From the period we spent in Antwerp, I also remember almost nothing, apart from several horrendous events I experienced two years later. We were hiding at the time in some kind of warehouse with many other refugees like ourselves. Suddenly, a fierce air raid began and the warehouse collapsed. Everything went up in flames. To my right and to my left entire families were lying on the ground, writhing in pools of their own blood. Beside me stood an injured woman; her clothing was torn; she was holding a small boy by the hand; blood was pouring from his wounds. The woman was screaming horribly. My parents and I escaped that incident unscathed. All around me people were lying on the ground in utter bewilderment. My parents clung fiercely to each other and to me, while I continued to stare at the scene as if I were sitting in a movie theater. I had no sense of catastrophe. Things happened and that was that. I felt only great sorrow at what I had witnessed, but I immediately recovered. I remember clearly that after that terrible explosion my parents held me so tightly that I was unable to extricate myself from their embrace for several minutes. It was only years later that I understood that my parents' enormous force was an expression of the intense relief they felt that all three of us were alive. But, what I remember is the pain and that more than anything I wished to release myself from their hold. I wanted only to move among the dead and wounded and to scrutinize them with a kind of fascinated curiosity in the midst of all the horror.

My parents were often annoyed by what they coined my "sick" curiosity when, for example, I tried to get up close to take a good look at people who had been wounded or even killed. I remember a train journey, probably the move from Antwerp to Brussels, when, all of a sudden, German soldiers travelling in the opposite direction started to take pot shots at us — behavior that could only be construed as having fun. The German soldiers were sitting in open rail cars and laughing hysterically. As the shots were being fired, my father was spread-eagled with his full body on top of Mother and me. When the shots stopped my parents' agitation was palpable and they didn't stop hugging me. I think I was also affected but as soon as it was all over, I was already busily checking the situation in the rail car, curious to see if anyone else had been hurt. For me it had been an extraordinary experience, a borderline game, and I am not sure that I didn't feel some wicked pleasure as I watched it being played out. I scanned my fellow passengers and with considerable interest and disbelief, I spotted a family that was sitting two rows behind us: a mother, a father and three children — two boys and a girl — all of whom were older than me. Their heartrending cries cut through the air, however no one approached them as every family was involved with itself.

I was absolutely mesmerized by the sight of that family. It was obvious that the father had been killed and the oldest girl appeared badly wounded. The two remaining sons were crying and the mother was obliged to deal with the situation. She didn't shed a single tear; her face was expressionless — stony — as if she was feeling no pain, whilst trying to muster all her strength in order to take control of the situation. I approached them and started to help her pick things up and to try to get the boys, who were grasping their mother tightly, to sit down. Very slowly people began to gather their wits. Anyone who hadn't been hurt, or whose family had not been hurt, moved forward to offer help, my father and mother, too. Everyone looked horrified except the mother. She continued to move quietly and precisely, almost automatically.

We stayed in Antwerp for two years, maybe two-and-a-half, and then, shortly after the outbreak of war, we moved to Brussels. Uncle Salo and Aunt Hanna'le came with us. I don't remember the exact date and or even the circumstances of our departure. When we set out on our journey of escape from Vienna, three of my mother's brothers were with us, but we subsequently parted ways. Salo and Hanna'le travelled with us to Antwerp, while the two other brothers, Paul and Latzo, left us in Antwerp and managed, after a long and tortuous journey, to reach America.

My parents and I in Antwerp, March 1940.

\* \* \*

Paul was married and was the father of a 12-month-old daughter. In late 1939, after the outbreak of war, he and his family succeeded in crossing France and arrived in the south. From there, they crossed the border to Spain and, after some time, they arrived in Casablanca, where they lived for about a year. They were then fortunate enough to make it to America. Although penniless and destitute, they had managed to save their own lives. They set up home in New York and had two more children. Uncle Paul was an extraordinary person — optimistic, dynamic, always on the move, full of faith and with a complete acceptance of life and a permanent naïve smile. Uncle Paul's life was an odyssey that was full of upheavals and disappointments, but he always continued to move forward. His ability to improvise was endless; he always found a solution to everything; he always knew how to get himself out of the many difficult situations that weighed down his life. He managed to raise a beautiful family and overcame all the obstacles he encountered along the way. Although he didn't succeed in building something that would provide him with a life of peace and tranquility, he always managed to remain in high spirits and content.

His wife, Gretchen, also from Vienna, was the daughter of an opera singer. She was a pretty, well-groomed woman, with playful eyes and long, flowing titian hair. She had the theatrical mannerisms of a successful actress, a diva, and her husband, Paul, worshipped the ground she walked on. I sometimes wondered how they had managed to escape from Belgium, to cross the European continent, to exist under extremely harsh conditions and to survive. I know that my parents, too, tried to get to the Land of Israel or to America, but they did not succeed. I think that there was an element of misfortune in their story; anyway, people develop special tools and mechanisms when they are at the edge of the abyss. It seems that my Uncle Paul's special qualities helped him cope with events and overcome them. Paul managed to survive with the help of his natural sensory system, and he made it to his desired destination. As for Gretchen, she, too, had a very special personality. For her, life was, to a large extent, a stage.

She was able to live it and at the same time to observe it as if it were an interesting theatrical production. She was also a strong woman, and this combination, together with the couple's unique relationship, brought them infinite success.

My mother's second brother, Latzo, also saved his and his wife's lives by escaping to America. I remember him as a strong and stable person, with both feet firmly on the ground. As a young man, he had been a boxer and by all accounts he had been a very opinionated and determined man. Physically, he was broad-shouldered, upright and solid. He had wide cheekbones and a direct gaze, always alert and ready to take on any situation and any conflict. He was quite different from Paul, who had a slim, wiry and sharp figure, with jerky and unpredictable movements. Latzo was a large taciturn man, but it was obvious that they were both spirited people. Latzo did well in New York. Both brothers were warm-hearted and devoted family men.

My grandfather Herman (my mother's father), died in Vienna after World War I. He had been a soldier in the Austrian Army and was injured in one of the last battles of the war. The story was that he died of an infection that developed as a result of the injury. My grandmother, Helen, who was referred to by everybody by her Hebrew name, Yocheved, managed to make it to the Land of Israel in 1938 to join her eldest son, Avshalom, who had gone as a pioneer in the 1920s. She was a short woman with a broad stocky figure and a very energetic and bubbly personality. People saw her as a hard, controlling and stubborn woman, a panther as a mother and grandmother and held in awe by her children and daughters-in-law; nonetheless, she enjoyed the respect of everyone who knew her. Grandmother Yocheved lived in Haifa and later in Jerusalem. In 1949, shortly after the establishment of the State of Israel, she decided to leave the country and join her sons in New York. In fact, she had been miserable in Israel, where she had never quite felt at home as she remained loyal to the lifestyle she had been used to in Vienna. She had never really learned Hebrew and left the new state as soon she could.

Avshalom's wife, Pnina, was a noble woman who devoted all her life to helping others. She never ceased to be amazed by anything her husband did that characterized Grandmother Yocheved's relationship with her children. For example, during those harsh pre-State of Israel years, Avshalom lived with his family in Haifa and paid frequent visits to his mother. On those trips, he would bring her the necessary ingredients to bake her favorite babka cake exactly as she had done in Vienna. For the taste to be just right, it was necessary to use butter, an ingredient that was in short supply and was carefully rationed to children only. Avshalom, the loving and devoted son, wanted to spare his mother the painful shortage suffered by many of the population in those days of austerity, and did his best to provide her with the "atmosphere" of her Viennese home and to make her life in Israel more comfortable. He, therefore, took his children's butter ration and gave it to his mother. The story of Grandmother's babka cake left her modest and generous daughter-in-law, Pnina, with a bitter taste in her mouth.

Avshalom was Grandmother Yocheved's first-born son. He worked hard for years until there was no longer any work available and had no choice but to return to Vienna, where he lived for a few years. In 1935, he returned to the Land of Israel. He was a true idealist — he helped to clear the swamps in the Hula valley and elsewhere and contributed to building the country whilst demanding nothing for himself. He was a genuine liberal, a modest and naïve person, and didn't have an ounce of evil in his body. Pnina and Avshalom raised two extremely successful sons, my cousins, and to this day, I feel very close to them.

\* \* \*

It was in Brussels that the real hunt began, and it was there that we began our period of wandering. After leaving Antwerp, my parents rented an apartment in quite a handsome bourgeois-style building on 56 Avenue du Roi, an elegant Brussels boulevard in the Saint-Gilles neighborhood. It was a wide boulevard with a dense row of tall trees down its center, which gave the area an aristocratic look, even though its other end bordered on the city's southern railway station and a rather low-class neighborhood. The German Army made a habit of parading its troops along the length of this boulevard, with soldiers marching in perfect order along the avenue's middle lane and singing at the tops of their voices, drawing large numbers of Belgian onlookers who lauded and applauded them. There were many quiet observers as well, whose faces showed signs of concern.

Our new apartment consisted of a large bedroom and a living room that doubled as a dining room. In the center of the room stood a big oblong table around which our lives were conducted. Strangely, I have no recollection of where I slept in that apartment; whether I had a room of my own, whether I continued to sleep in my parents' room, or whether I slept in the living room. But it wasn't long before we were obliged to leave this handsome apartment. The Gestapo, or regular German soldiers who conducted endless searches in the area, had arrived at our building. From then on, my parents rented only small apartments in which we could live anonymously, with no need for any kind of registration. It was for this reason, too, that my parents chose to rent single rooms in the attics of apartment blocks. Separately from us, my uncle and aunt also conducted their lives in the same way; they tried to rent apartments near us, which enabled us to meet frequently. Throughout that period, they were the only people we met. I loved them very much. Whenever we were able to return to our permanent apartment on the Avenue du Roi I was happy. But within a few weeks we'd be forced, once again, to flee for our lives and go on the run for a few months, until our landlord could inform us that the neighborhood was quiet and we could return home — until the next time.

In each of the apartments we inhabited, we were able to draw a kind of boundary, separating the outside world from our own family life and I felt protected. Inside the apartment the atmosphere was always cozy and warm even during the cold winter days. At those times, despite the severe tension we were constantly under and the moves from apartment to apartment, I knew what it was like to have a genuine family life and I often caught myself smiling happily. These were hope-filled days. Occasionally, we would go out, step into the street, and be swallowed up for a time by the harsh world outside, but we always knew there was somewhere to return to. My happiness during that period of my life, which I remember as wonderful, because

I was surrounded by people who loved me — my parents, my beloved uncle and his beautiful wife — was accompanied by a kind of anxiety; I felt as if it was all too good to be true. I would dive into the embracing softness of my happiness, my sense of security, of complacency, but somewhere inside me I knew that danger was lurking. Time after time, reality reshuffled the cards and forced us to escape from the constant manhunts that took place in the area or in the building we lived in and we found ourselves once again in a dark, one-room apartment, forced yet again to recreate an atmosphere of home.

One afternoon, Mother and I were taking an excursion on a cable car. Suddenly, two armed German soldiers boarded the carriage and checked the documents of each of the passengers. I don't remember if we were wearing our yellow stars on that occasion, but the soldiers lingered beside my mother and eventually ordered us to disembark from the car. On the street, they pushed us with the butts of their rifles and pointed us in the direction of some place we were unfamiliar with. My mother held my hand so hard that it hurt. She was tense, determined and grim and I was certain we were in trouble. It was a period of many arrests and we knew it wasn't a good omen, possibly even a very bad one. However, suddenly, something unexpected attracted the attention of the soldiers. They appeared somewhat troubled and, after exchanging a few brief sentences, and without warning, they broke into a run and disappeared. My mother and I stood motionless, like statues. We were paralyzed and for a few moments we were unable to sever our feet from the ground on which we stood. And then, possibly for the very first time, I was gripped by a terrible fear and burst into uncontrollable tears. My mother cried too, but she quickly pulled herself together and realized that we had to get away from that place and disappear, in case we drew unnecessary attention to ourselves in an unfamiliar location. She also feared the return of the soldiers. So, we made off quickly and returned home exhausted and utterly despondent.

Fear was usually unfamiliar to me. First of all, when we were moving house frequently, I probably had a kind of toughness that helped me cope with difficult situations and now I was suddenly feeling as if something inside me had weakened. I didn't discuss it with my parents, because I had a clear sense that it was my job to solve my own problems. Before this incident we had often coped with sensitive and even difficult situations, but I don't remember feeling fear. However, I do remember that my parents were frightened and expressed their anxiety, but I was not afraid.

Mr. Hourmont, our landlord at 56 Avenue du Roi, was a fairly prosperous merchant or businessman and he owned the entire building. His family, which consisted of himself, his wife and his only son, Guy, lived on the ground floor of the building, or, to be more accurate, on a kind of half story below the ground floor. The lower level of the apartment had windows, through the upper part of which it was possible to see the sidewalks outside. I don't know why they chose to live in this particular apartment; maybe so as to rent out the other apartments in the building, or perhaps it was the safest place in the building when the city was being bombed from the air. Mr. Hourmont was a good man, although not overly sociable or warm. He was quite introverted, somewhat grumpy, didn't talk much and didn't look you in the eye when he spoke. Still, he was a strong, principled man and, most importantly, he was reliable. Physically, he was short and chubby and moved heavily, but he was dynamic and reminded me of Winston Churchill, Britain's wartime Prime Minister and our unchallenged hero. Mrs. Hourmont was a gentle lady, pleasant and quiet. She spent most of her time sitting in a wide armchair covered by a thick blanket with a book in her hand. She was probably very sick. Her hands and face were covered with sores and she died during the war, or shortly afterwards. Their son, Guy, was six or seven years older than me, short for his age and chubby. I don't know what he knew about us — whether he didn't know that we were Jews, or whether his father had instructed him to keep secret the fact that we were Jews and were living in his father's building.

At that time, my Aunt Hanna'le and Uncle Salo, who were living in a nearby building, taught me to ride a bicycle. If we ever noticed a German soldier, not to mention a group of German soldiers, we would try to slip away as quickly as possible, avoiding any eye contact with them. We were nimble and thoroughly practiced and we always managed to get away in time.

Around 1942, I believe, we began having to wear the yellow star pinned to our lapel. We were forbidden to spend time outside without it and on the occasions when we removed it, we would avoid questions or casual conversation with Germans. When we were wearing the yellow star, we were acting in accordance with the law, but we never knew whether changes had been made to the racist, anti-Jewish regulations. Many Jews were captured on the streets because of the yellow stars they wore on their lapels, since the stars made it easier to identify them. There were also random laws; every now and then an order was issued to attack all Jews in a specific neighborhood and under these circumstances it was advisable to be as far away as possible from the eyes of the Gestapo, who were dressed in civilian clothing. Even the Belgian police was better avoided. This uncertainty forced us into a state of permanent insecurity.

We were well aware that we were prisoners in the hands of our landlord and we hoped he would continue to behave fairly towards us. And so it was. Mr. Hourmont often warned us of searches being made in the area and hence, we would be forced to leave the place for a few hours, days or sometimes for several months. It all happened between 1941 and March 1943 and I was six or seven at the time. In 1943, I was separated from my parents for the last time.[7] Mr. Hourmont did his utmost to protect us; he was discreet, asked no questions, and always warned my parents against leaving the house, especially at night. The man risked his own life for our sakes. There is no doubt that he is worthy of great respect for his courage and for adhering to his principles and maintaining his humanity under such harsh circumstances.

I know that during our stay in Mr. Hourmont's building I started going to school, but for some reason, I remember very little of this chapter in my life. Occasionally, pictures of myself in school spring

---

7   The mass round-ups of Jews for deportation to Poland began in mid-July 1942, initially in Antwerp then in Brussels. The first transport to the East departed from Belgium on August 4, 1942. Forty-five percent of Belgium's Jews were exterminated in Auschwitz.

to mind, alongside my mother's reservations about the wisdom of sending me there. She would sometimes say that it would be better if I didn't go to school "under these uncertain circumstances." On rare occasions, I would play with one or two boys outside, but always nearby. Once, when I was playing in the avenue in front of the building, I fell off a bench and broke my arm at the elbow. Had it only been a matter of a broken bone, I wouldn't even mention it here, but under the circumstances, everything changed and I remember the incident as highly traumatic. It appeared to be a serious fracture and I was required to spend two weeks in hospital. I had two or three operations, in the course of which the doctors inserted a nail into the injured elbow. I subsequently spent several days in bed with my arm raised and connected to some instrument, and small, colorful (mainly blue and red) blisters appeared around the elbow.

For years afterwards, I asked myself how my parents had succeeded in those days of escape and hiding to keep me in a Brussels hospital. The reply to this came only a few years ago, when I received a parcel of letters written after the liberation of Belgium and shortly before the end of the war. It was correspondence relating to me between Mr. Hourmont, Aunt Angele and my family in Israel. In one of those letters, Mr. Hourmont wrote that in 1942 I broke a bone in my arm and he took me, together with my mother, to the hospital and they registered me as his son. This knowledge did even more to increase my respect for that courageous man.

I was very lonely and quite afraid in the hospital, as well as being aware of my special situation. I tried to overcome the pain and to attract as little attention as possible to myself. However, while in the hospital, I befriended a young nurse who was working on my ward. She was pretty and fair-skinned, with a smile that rarely left her face. I was extremely lonely then because my parents were unable to visit me often. Whenever the young nurse was able to take a few minutes off her busy work schedule, she would come and sit by my bed and, sometimes, she'd hold my healthy hand. She often played various kinds of role-play games with me, in which we had to assume different identities and get into their skins as if it was real. I became a shop assistant, a building worker, a policeman, a soldier or an old man with restricted movement and verbal abilities. She usually took on female roles — a mother, grandmother, my older sister, my younger sister.

We would get very involved in our roles, laughing or crying as we got angry with or complained about each other…it was theater at its best. To a large extent, these performances relieved me of tension. I was obliged to concentrate on the roles I had chosen, to characterize them and to find ways to present them in a convincing manner. When the nurse was off duty, or when she was busy with her work, I had to think about and invent all kinds of stories for the next time she had a spare moment to come and visit me. I felt that she, too, was interested in these visits because she was also reassured by those games of ours, unless I am mistaken and she played them only out of sympathy and pity for a lonely little boy. I often surprised her with my ideas and there were even incidents when she was left speechless in the course of our conversations, since I had more time than her to prepare. I used to learn my part well and tried to imagine how she would react and respond. She, on the other hand, always had to improvise on the spot. We used to fall about in laughter when our conversations led to a dead end.

Her company made it possible for me to while away the time pleasantly and also to considerably improve my French language skills, and the role-play games provided me with an escape from my grim reality. During those moments I created and inhabited another world in which I placed only two characters: my nurse and I. It was a hermetically sealed world reserved just for the two of us. We were on a desert island, dreaming our dreams.

One day, my parents appeared at the hospital with Salo and Hanna'le. While I was trying to arouse their sympathy and show them how much I was suffering, I noticed a look of despair on all four faces. They tried to explain that Salo and Hanna'le had to go away. Although they promised to return soon, their explanations for having to leave were filled with a profound sadness. I felt they were trying to hide something from me but I was too involved with my own issues at that moment and didn't give the matter enough thought. Salo hugged and kissed me. Hanna'le hugged me tightly and her lips murmured something that sounded like, "Why don't I have a son like you?" Later, whenever I thought about Hanna'le, I often remembered the way she used to look at me, with a sad, maternal softness in her eyes and it was obvious that she yearned for a child. That was the last time I ever saw them.

Several years later, I learned that they had received a notice to report to the Belgian army camp in the town of Malines, located between Antwerp and Brussels.[8] The order had come from the Belgian police. It later transpired that it had been a ruse on the part of the Gestapo to draw the Jews into a trap, with no complications. The Belgian police collaborated with the Gestapo and provided the bait. A few days after their departure, Salo and Hanna'le somehow succeeded in getting a message through to my parents that they had been tricked.

My uncle and aunt travelled to Malines not knowing what awaited them, although from the expressions on their faces and on those of my parents, too, they clearly had a premonition that something bad was going to happen. It was a time in which persecution of the Jews was intensifying. Perhaps my uncle and aunt were suspicious of the objective behind the police directive they had received, but they were probably afraid to admit to themselves what really awaited them and hence, reported as demanded at the required place and time. The camp at Malines was in fact a transit camp; on August 11, 1942 Salo and Hanna'le were transported from there to Auschwitz.

I often recalled the last meeting I had with my Uncle Salo and Aunt Hanna'le. For many years I suffered from the "undignified" way in which we parted ways. I was so involved with myself and my own minor problems and was so oblivious to everyone else's feelings that I was unable to acknowledge their hints that this meeting was not like

---

8    Twenty-five thousand Jews were sent to the Malines transit camp for transportation to Auschwitz. Wishing at first to avoid police involvement, the Germans ordered the Jewish Council (or AJB) to send official letters to individual members of the Jewish community with instructions to "report for work" in northern France and the East. When the Jews refused, the Germans conducted mass round-ups with the aid of German police forces, which were assisted by local volunteers. Belgian community or municipal police forces were employed between July and August 1942 in Antwerp only.

any other. This was not the first meeting and was certainly not the last to cause me such deep feelings of distress.

When I recall the times in which I took my leave of people who were dear to me in an atmosphere that was somewhat "gloomy," I feel the stab of a missed opportunity. I wish I could erase it all and start again; such a loss leaves one with a persistent restlessness. This feeling continues to be oppressive even so many years later, taking me back with amazing accuracy to the very moment it happened and increases the pain of the loss. This emotionally-charged memory gives me no rest. I often think of Salo and Hanna'le and my thoughts always lead me to that last meeting. I gave this parting serious thought as a youth, after the war had ended. In my thoughts I conjured up "alternatives" to this parting of ways and always managed to improve the end, to the extent that reality and imagination began to mingle and I often didn't know what was true and what wasn't. However, the feeling that remains as strong as ever is that of guilt and a missed opportunity.

The greatest pain comes from the knowledge that they responded immediately to the call from the police. It was a kind of inexplicable suicide. In one of his letters, Mr. Hourmont describes how he tried to dissuade them from reporting to the camp at Malines. They could have escaped rather than "volunteer" and made their own way to the end of their lives. Or, perhaps, they would have survived. It is quite clear to me that Salo and Hanna'le — like many other Jews — refused to believe in the reality of death. They must have had their doubts, if I am to judge by the looks on their faces on that visit to me in hospital. Or maybe they believed that they would be saved if they behaved in accordance with the instructions they received, and what could be more natural than to report for duty when you are called to do so by the authorities?

# CHAPTER TWO

## *AUNT ANGELE*

"Come, Harry, come sit with us," my father called me one afternoon. "Your mother and I want to discuss things with you." The expression on my parents' faces was extremely grim and they appeared to be under great pressure. I got out of bed, advanced slowly towards the large dining table that filled the room's space and sat down on one of the chairs. Father, who did his utmost to control his voice, continued, "You know how much we love you and how good it has been here for the three of us together. However, as you can see, we are not living in normal times and the most important thing now is for us to get through this period as quietly and safely as possible. This war won't last much longer and we must organize our lives in such a way as to ensure that we shall reunite when it is over." He paused for a moment, as if trying to understand whether I was aware of what he meant. I tried to follow his words, but I could feel my thoughts wandering and I only nodded my head in agreement.

Mother was watching me with enormous sadness. Father, who chose his words meticulously, appeared determined. From the sad tone of his words, I was able to understand that something was happening and that there was no contradicting him. Father drew a deep breath and continued, "In times such as these, it is sometimes best to separate for a while. It is safer. In the end, when it is all over, we shall all be together once again. Do you understand?" I did not reply and he went on to say, "We have found a good home for you with a nice lady called Aunt Angele. She has a son who is ten years older than you. He will be a kind of big brother to you. You will do well with them. You'll be able to go to school like all the other children and you'll have lots of friends. We'll visit you once a week, but no more, because visits of this kind are dangerous, to you as well as to us. As long as you are with Aunt Angele, you'll have to live under an assumed name. You will become a Belgian Christian boy, like all the friends you'll make there. Aunt Angele will teach you all their customs and you'll behave like everyone else. You must never mention that you are Jewish. You have to just behave like all the other neighborhood children. In this way, you'll be able to live a more liberated life and will no longer have to hide. You'll have to make sure to follow Aunt Angele's advice, because you'll be living with her and from now on she'll be the one to tell you what to do." Father stopped there for a moment. His tone softened and became very intimate and he whispered quietly but with great force, "Behave like every other Christian boy, but deep, deep in your heart, remember that you are a Jew. And even if everything that is happening to us now is because we are Jews, we must remain loyal to our forefathers. Don't forget what I am telling you. Soon, when all this is over, we shall once again live together happily." Mother said nothing but every one of Father's words was confirmed further by the expression on her face. It was March 1943, two or three days after my eighth birthday, and I realized that I was unable to refuse.

Hence, I arrived in a house in a Brussels suburb. A tall upright woman welcomed us and invited us in before closing the door carefully behind her. A heavy silence hung all around. The landlady smiled at us and suggested politely that we sit down but we remained standing. Father began by introducing us, "This is Aunt Angele. You'll be living here in her house for a while. We'll soon come to visit you." He hugged me quickly and turned his back on me. My mother followed him. In a choked voice she said, "My dear boy. Don't worry. We'll meet again soon. Be a good boy and do as Aunt Angele tells you." They quickly shook the landlady's hand, opened the door carefully and slipped out into the darkness. I remained standing next to Aunt Angele. Her large eyes scrutinized me benevolently. From that moment things moved quickly.

I looked all around me. I was standing in a large, warm living room that was very different from those I had known during our last few years. We had lived sparsely, in apartments lacking all charm, but I felt wonderful in them because I was with my parents and their presence instilled in me a sense of warmth and calm. That day, the rain smashed fiercely against the large windowpanes and I felt an overwhelming exhaustion, emptiness and a dreadful loneliness. What am I doing here, in this strange and beautiful place? I don't belong among all this grandeur. A powerful loneliness engulfed me. There, I sat all alone, devoid of all purpose, with no support, without the familiar faces of the people I loved. I was filled with a sad desperation; I felt weak and vulnerable.

Aunt Angele asked me to remain in the living room while she prepared my room. I looked around me. The floor was almost entirely covered by a soft thick carpet, embroidered with a plethora of flowers and leaves in dark muted colors. Hanging on the walls were several portraits of elegantly dressed people, looking me straight in the eye arrogantly. But what most captured my attention was a large wall clock that emitted a loud, but tender and caressing sound. The sound pleased my ears and may have somewhat dulled my frame of mind. It sounded friendly and was the first thing I connected to in this new place. The second thing that caught my eye was a small oil painting hanging next to the clock. The painting depicted a rural scene that appeared familiar and I felt at ease looking at it. My eyes continued to roam around the room and the walls in search of other objects I could connect with. As I was searching, Aunt Angele entered and informed me that my room was ready and that I could go up with my suitcase and get myself organized. It was my first night alone without my father and mother. I lay down and, while I wondered what my new life would be like, I fell asleep.

I knew that the following day I would be turning over a new page in my life and so it was. My name was changed, I adopted a new identity and my life took a different turn. I was forced to adopt a mode of behavior that was appropriate to my new circumstances. When I arrived at Aunt Angele's I was aware that my former family framework had completely fallen apart. Therefore, I accepted Aunt Angele's favors and was very eager to blend into my new environment. I developed an almost obsessive yearning to be just like everyone else. The trouble lay in the fact that I had no one with whom to share these feelings. Even then, I was trying to understand the significance of a family framework and its importance in the lives of human beings. Why did the routine of life, at which everyone was so eager to scoff, appear to me to be the elixir of life, without which it is so hard to exist? Even then, I felt the beauty that is in routine, harmony and stability. Routine is symbolic of the scheme of customs in which mankind feels at home; it is an expression of warmth and intimacy and is a safe foundation for everything that is familiar to us.

Until then the routine of my life had been one of danger, terror and wandering, but it contained love, concern and a mutual pledge, which managed to instill in me a sense of security wherever I was. My parents were my home; they provided me with a wall of safety. Now, I had moved to a different life routine. It was the beginning of a journey into the unknown, on my own, without the security I had, until then, been able to rely upon. What did the future hold in store for me? The routine of my new life was built on the ruins of the routine I had known with my parents and my separation from them involved a great deal of pain. But, even then, and perhaps against a background of my mother's reassuring promises, I awaited it with hope, I even yearned for it. It was my chance to be like all the other children. I was equipped with a new identity; one that had belonged to a dead Belgian boy of my age (so they told me at the time), and my name from then on was to be Henri Dieudonné, born in 1935 in the Belgian town of Namur.

In my new home we were able to establish a relatively stable and organized routine, in which I found my own place. For this, I credit Aunt Angele, who was a warm, sensitive and goodhearted woman. She tried hard to create for me a pleasant environment in order to fill the void left by my mother and father. René, Aunt Angele's son, the third rib in this new family framework, was frequently away from home, and a few months after my arrival, he was recruited into the Belgian Army and we didn't see him again. So my new family quickly became just two people, Aunt Angele and myself. In spite of the severe food shortage, she managed to serve good meals, which were as palatable as they were pleasing to the eye. We always tried to eat our evening meals together, with each of us sitting in his regular place and we even conducted our conversations on regular subjects. Very gradually, I became accustomed to my new lifestyle and began to feel at ease with my new identity.

I learned to recite my new credentials. If I was awakened in the middle of the night and asked my name, I had no trouble providing my new name and the history of my "family." I learned everything a Christian child was supposed to know about Christianity — the customs, the prayers and the rituals of the Church. From the very beginning, I understood that there was a big difference between acting like a Christian and actually feeling like one. I took into account that, at first, I would attract considerable attention among the congregation of the small neighborhood church, until I became a natural part of the congregation that I so wanted to be a part of. I strove for this in two ways: The first consisted of self-persuasion. Christianity is better than Judaism; the fact is that only Jews are harassed, whereas Christians are allowed to conduct their lives in relative peace. Among the Christians, life goes on as usual. As a Jew, I have to hide, I can't speak my mother tongue, I live under an identity that is not mine, I am obliged to live separately from my parents and I must live in permanent fear. This, as I have already mentioned, was the first stage. I devoted much time and constant thought to that self-persuasion and decided to adopt the demeanor of a Christian. I was aware of the fact that my behavior was usually different from that of a non-Jewish child, but this was not enough. I tried to become integrated into the environment, to be unobtrusive, to be careful, to behave with restraint and to consider my responses cautiously and with a cool mind.

In actual fact, my behavior was that of an adult. I felt that I was different and not like others, but I knew that I had no other choice and that I had to conform if I was to survive. However, aside from considerations of survival, I felt a deep need to be like everyone else, to feel good in my skin, to look people in the eye, to walk in the street with my head held high, rather than looking down, as I had done when I wore the yellow Star of David on my breast. I had always longed to hide that symbol, to make it disappear from sight, and now, although it was no longer on the lapel of my coat, it had not completely disappeared. I felt my new personality gradually evolving. The decision "to work on myself" on every level of my existence, alongside the changes I had undergone, gave me strength from within. Together, the two left their mark on me and achieved impressive results.

My new language — French — suddenly became fluent and this fluency increased my self-confidence. Even my walk became more determined. Sometimes, I would find myself scrutinizing my new external self and became aware of the changes my behavior had undergone on the outside. It was fascinating, but also strange. The changes in me even affected my attitude toward the German soldiers who were to be found at every turn. Whenever I came upon one my feeling was of some kind of security and I felt no fear. The anxieties had disappeared and were replaced with a strong urge for revenge, to cause them harm, to humiliate them and to show them that I was no longer afraid of them. But there was no one with whom I was able to share this feeling of victory. However, Aunt Angele felt the change that was taking place in me. She noticed my arrogance vis-à-vis the occupier, the self-confidence that filled me and she concluded that this state of mind would only lead to trouble.

Shortly after my arrival at Aunt Angele's, I befriended a group of French-speaking Belgian Walloon children. The choice had not been random. First of all, the French speakers all lived in the vicinity of Aunt Angele's house. At a distance of two or three streets away, there was a community of Belgian Flemish, whose language was mainly Flemish, although they all spoke fluent French as well. Even though my French was still stilted at the time and my mother tongue,

German, was closer to Flemish, it was obvious to me that I belonged to the French-speaking group. My new name and identity also dictated my choice of peer group — the Walloons.[9]

Relations were more or less good between the Flemish and the Walloon families, but not so among the children. My new friends were about my age; some were older. I was eight years old when I arrived at Aunt Angele's and several of the group members were nine, ten or even eleven. I was initiated into the Walloon "ethnic gang" that had declared war on another ethnic group — the Flemish. It would be more accurate to say that the Flemish group was the one that declared war on the Walloons. At that time, the Walloons were part of a higher social class. For example, I noticed that most of the house cleaners came from the Flemish community. It was something of a class war and the children's behavior somewhat reflected the attitudes of their parents. As soon as I became a part of the French "gang" I was identified with them. For me, this was an extraordinarily successful healing process. I was much less involved with myself — in the way I looked and in the impression I made on my surroundings. For the first time in my life, I was part of something. I belonged to a group whose identity and mission happened to have been based on an ethnic issue, but, as far as I was concerned, it could have been anything.

For the first time, I experienced the feeling of participation, of belonging to a group in which I also played a role; I was no longer living on the periphery of life — I was in the middle, with a bunch of others. I wasn't used to being among so many people and tended at first to keep quiet, both because of my problems with the language and because of Aunt Angele's warnings, but gradually I began to feel comfortable and was able to voice my opinions and hence, my French improved

9   Straddling the cultural boundary between Germanic and Latin Europe, Belgium is home to two main linguistic groups – the Dutch speakers who are mainly Flemish and the French speakers who are mainly Walloons, with an additional small group of German speakers. Belgium's two largest regions are the Dutch-speaking northern region of Flanders and the French-speaking southern region of Wallonia. To this day, Brussels remains a French-speaking enclave with a Flemish minority. The spread of language also represents a national divide.

significantly. I felt strange at first, expressing myself in public with dozens of pairs of eyes watching me intently. I had no brothers or sisters and I had never before had any friends. Everything that was happening to me at that time was primeval, primary. Although I was discovering the world several years too late and was rubbing shoulders with people who were quite strange to me, I learned to find my place in society.

At the time, the word "society" made me smile. I had never been to nursery school. Although I had attended school when I was six, I had very few memories from that time, since I had been absent more frequently than I had been present. Now, for the first time, at the age of eight, I started to attend school (here, too, I was absent a lot but I still managed to learn a little) and to meet a few fellow classmates with whom I also played after school. In addition, I went to church and there, too, I met other children. In the end, the group of French-speaking Walloon kids became the most important thing in my life at that time. Each one found his place in the group on the strength of his presence, personality, power and craftiness. We each had to create our own position in the group and to secure it. There was a natural leadership in the form of an eleven-year-old boy. I don't remember his name and his appearance, too, has faded from my memory during the many years that have passed since. Nonetheless, his image as a leader has remained deeply carved in my memory. It was the first time in my life that I saw a person (not necessarily a child) who managed, on the strength of his charisma, to be accepted unequivocally as the leader of a non-homogenous group, to breathe new life into it, to arouse in each and every one of them solidarity and a willingness to fight for something that was not entirely clear.

Although they heard at home about the inequality between the two ethnic groups that formed the population of Belgium, this was not the only explanation, especially since there was a war being fought all around that did not make things any easier. Each child had his own reasons of course, but most of them would turn up to fight in order to discharge the enormous tension that infused the city and the school and was especially apparent within their homes. Moreover, the uniqueness of the times meant that children had more liberty. Those childish scuffles were very enjoyable and interaction with other children often came at the expense of spending time with family, which, in any case, had a volatile atmosphere. Many of the fathers were absent and the mothers found it hard to control their children as well as they should. So, for us, this group provided a substitute for family life.

There were some harsh exchanges of blows between us and some of us were injured and went home bruised, bleeding and with broken bones. We even carried simple, but pain-inducing "weapons," such as sticks, sometimes even quite solid ones, stones, clubs and ropes that we used for tying up prisoners. On the other hand, as soon as the battle was over, we'd all walk home quietly together, Flemish and Walloon children as one. There was a kind of code of behavior and we acted in accordance with it and never strayed from it. Often, we witnessed the acceptance of serious deviations from international rules of war in the world around us. We frequently proclaimed to ourselves that this war would have looked quite different had the adults agreed to observe us and to learn from us how to fight, while maintaining a generous chivalry.

When a juvenile Flemish fighter happened to be on the same street as a juvenile Walloon fighter, they would not engage in conversation; they would make do with a light wave of the hand as a symbol of peace, after which each would go his own way. As a greeting, it was an expression of respect between warriors on both sides of the barricade. Occasionally, when a Flemish and a Walloon child found themselves standing next to each other in a queue, for example, they would go so far as to start a conversation. They would exchange niceties and make small talk, but never mention the war between them. There was respect for a fighter who was stern but honest. Later, I tried to understand how, as children, we had managed to create such a world, a world that was stubborn, yet had values, which didn't slip into the abyss of hostility so typical of our parents' generation. I understood then that the world of children was prepared to make compromises because it was reserving some kind of hope, whereas the adults no longer were.

Once, in a fight that had turned particularly violent, the Flemish children were winning. Some of the Walloons were injured and so we decided to withdraw. In that battle I must have been on the frontline and when I tried to escape with the others I was overcome by a few of the

Flemish children and beaten to a pulp. I was then taken prisoner, tied up with a thick rope and held like that for several hours. They beat me, albeit not very hard, and made use mainly of psychological pressure that took the form of threats. It was a very humiliating situation, but, since all's fair in love and war, these were the rules of the game. I hoped the Walloons would come to my rescue.

The Flemish children, who were prepared for a counterattack, left two of their fighters standing guard over me. My hands were tied and I was helpless. Although the Walloons, in their attempt to release me, had flanked out around us and were already close to me, once again a stick and fist fight erupted between the two camps, the Flemish children gained the lead and the Walloons were forced to withdraw yet again. After two hours the enemy released me, just as the Walloons were about to storm the Flemish children yet again. They must have decided that they had had enough for the day and wanted to go home. My friends came over to me immediately, apologized for their failure to release me and everything went back to being the way it was.

This environment was extremely important to me. First of all, it was an effective cure for the sadness I was immersed in after realizing that my parents would not be coming back soon. It was also the first time to have friends, to have any kind of a presence among unfamiliar people; I was part of a group, I had a position. Apart from that, I participated in the attacks, too, and I initiated and acted towards an objective. Whereas, until then, I had only ever hidden and defended myself. And, finally, it helped me to form a new personality that I tried to design for myself and present to the world. I was like everyone else. No longer was I the hounded Jewish kid. I sang a song of praise to everything that wasn't Jewish. I was a gentile boy, like all the others, with a new identity and an independent personality. In the morning, I would look in the mirror to see if my hair had become lighter, if my eyes had turned blue, if I had managed to erase the sadness from my face. I felt wonderful in my new skin, with my new status as a member of a group of fighters and socially accepted by each and every one of them.

So the days passed. Nevertheless, alone with myself at night, I would return to my real, unadorned identity and it was then that the truth would hit me with full force: I am a Jew. "Henri, Henri, what's the matter with you?" I opened my eyes and saw Aunt Angele shaking her head in concern. "Henri, you were calling out anxiously in your sleep. At first, your face was all distorted and suddenly it appeared calm and a broad smile spread over your lips. What is going on in your brain at night?" What could I say? Could I tell her that in my sleep I was witnessing sweet revenge? She would think I had lost my mind. To be honest, I was quite crushed. I lay there exhausted with my eyes shut and my thoughts a long way away. I didn't reply to Aunt Angele, because what I really wanted was for her to leave the room. And she did. I was involved with myself and wished to be alone. I tried to return to the dream and to reconstruct the scenes I had just witnessed, but they had already dissolved. Could I be living in two worlds? The thought caused a shiver to run through me. Aunt Angele switched off the light and the room was shrouded in darkness. I looked around me. The world that surrounded me was friendly to me. It was a world that hovered between dream and reality. I was sometimes able to reenter a dream, but never to actually reenact each of the details and activities that had taken place in it. The room's darkness belonged to the intermediary world. It separated the real world from the world of dreams in which the important things happened, the heroic events that provided me with the strength to cope with the day-to-day.

My savior, Angele Cloof-Meuldermans. In June 1995, she was honored by Yad Vashem as a "Righteous Among the Nations."

A significant part of my life in those days took place in my dreams. It could even be said that I lived my life twice. First, my life took place in the daytime and then I relived it during the night. My dreams of revenge filled a void and provided me with satisfaction and a spiritual boost, which was in complete contrast with the grayness of everyone's lives. However, the distinction would disappear at times between the real and the imagined, between dream and reality. At times, it seemed that the boundaries became blurred. On one particular night, I dreamed of a German railway carriage being blown up with all its cargo. The explosion completely destroyed the train and killed all the German soldiers inside.

I was often visited by that figure Nathaniel. It was he, the fighter, who blew up the train together with his comrades. They were all Jews. It was a violent attack. The explosion shook the earth. Body parts of the German soldiers were flung far and wide. I saw flames and smoke and the smell of burning flesh filled my nostrils. I stood there hypnotized. Who was this Nathaniel? Suddenly, I felt that perhaps I was Nathaniel. It was certainly extremely real. And then, everything became clear and very logical. The tiredness was real. I had indeed taken part in an attack on a German train.

This act filled me with a sense of joy and fulfillment. I could return to my Jewishness, the Jewishness I had tried so hard to repress in my everyday life. Again, I was living a double life. During the day, I was in every sense a Walloon child and at night, I was a Jewish child thirsty for revenge. More and more frequently, almost every night, Nathaniel would appear in my room to help me cope with the terror that surrounded me from every quarter. However, the trouble with dreams, as everyone knows, is that the moment you awake, the leading characters fade away and any attempt to hold onto them is doomed to fail. In most cases, individual pictures remain etched on one's memory and make their winding way into the drawers of the soul, which appear to be awaiting them. Perhaps that's the reason that the image I dreamed about kept returning to me in exactly the same format — the same facial features and the same upright body; a larger than life biblical figure, impressive, yet a little frightening and at the same time, so very close. It was a hypnotic look that was simultaneously full of gentleness.

The name Nathaniel has been familiar to me forever. It is, after all, the Hebrew translation of my Belgian name — Dieudonné. My father's words took on real meaning: "Remember that you are a Jew. Remember that we are a heroic nation. Continue to be courageous." The meetings with Nathaniel gave me strength and restored some of my self-confidence. I felt good in his company and I often dreamed that, like him, I, too, would not surrender; that I, too, was punishing the Germans. The more frequent Nathaniel's visits became, the stronger was the bond I felt towards him and I gradually adopted him as my alter ego. So powerful was the solidarity I felt for his mission that often I was actually a part of it. Suddenly, it was me who was part of this assignment and carrying out all those daring deeds. When I opened my eyes, I would feel a surge of pleasant relief spreading through my limbs. I think I was also smiling. Aunt Angele would sometimes observe me with a puzzled look on her face, as if wondering what could possibly be happening to this boy.

Very carefully I opened my right eye. I tried to see the sunshine through my lashes and to see if it was going to be a cold and rainy day as often happened during this season. Still excited by the long night journey I had just returned from, far from the light and from Aunt Angele's scrutiny, I fashioned for myself a small dent in the bed, wrapped myself in my eiderdown and snuggled down into it. However, the enormous pride I felt was diluted by bitter depression. Again, I had awakened at the very moment when I should have been witnessing a fateful event. I felt I was involved in those nocturnal events, as if I had again taken part in them, as I had on all those nights when I dreamed my heroic dreams. I was still under the influence of those night sights; the figures had never seemed so real as they did this time. I tried my utmost to hold onto them in order to continue to be there, in that place, but they gradually slipped out of my grasp until they disappeared altogether. But my memory maintained several very powerful flashes that I was able to return to and reconstruct for days to come. The sight gave me renewed strength for quite a while and indicated some objective that remained carved in my mind.

Then, Aunt Angele would urge me to get up quickly and go to school. Things had been quiet lately and life was continuing peacefully.

About three times a week we had our fights with the Flemish children and the days began to resemble each other, creating a pleasant routine. The events of those months did nothing to undermine my inner stability; not even the nighttime events. I felt fresh and sure of myself. I was in an environment that I had begun to find familiar. I went to school almost every day like the other neighborhood children and at the end of every school day I would meet my friends with whom it was possible to cut loose and run wild, all without any adult supervision and without having anyone recite that sentence that I loathed: "It's dangerous for the Jews."

The church also began to play a significant role in my routine. I was quite charmed at that time by Catholicism and I tried to think a little about this issue that I found rather confusing. The new religion I had been obliged to adopt together with my new identity was definitely tempting. I liked the church's atmosphere of majestic splendor; I liked its sights, the adornments, the statues and the colorful pictures of saints. It was a world of imagination, somewhat mystical, with a great deal of beauty. The grand garments worn by the priests and the ceremony with which the mass was conducted captured my heart.

About six months after moving in with Aunt Angele, I was accepted into the church children's choir. We, too, wore colorful clothes — a red cloak over a white, lace-trimmed shirt. I often heard cries of wonder from the congregation, both at our singing and our dress and whispers such as, "Don't they look like angels?" I connected strongly with the image of an angel, a kind of utterly fabulous creature, with super-human properties and a child-like appearance. The church walls, too, were adorned with icons depicting little angels. We sang hymns in Latin in pure soprano voices and the sounds we emitted contributed to this image of angels that I was so attracted to. I enjoyed being a member of such a society, gaining respect from the church's congregation for being in the choir, as well as a spiritual boost.

As an adult, I often thought of the rich and varied life I had in those days. On the one hand, I was a member of a gang of "ruffians" whose only purpose was to beat their enemy; on the other hand, I belonged to a choir of angels whose sole concern was beauty and spirituality. Since I did not have a friend who was also a soulmate and into whose ears I could pour out my heart, I often did my soul-searching within myself.

Sometimes, I would take time out in order to organize my thoughts about my life and where it was going. I lived my life, but, at the same time, I observed it from the sidelines. There had already been many twists and turns in my life. For several years, I had lived with my parents in a form of complete isolation from the rest of the world; the only people I had known apart from my parents were Uncle Salo and Aunt Hanna'le. I had no doubt that I had been witness to some extremely significant events, but they constituted a chapter within some kind of agenda and gradually became a routine part of my life, part of the reality that I became accustomed to. Although I knew and played with some children at that time, I was forbidden to make friends with them. I had to be constantly alert and suspicious, to be aware and to hide. Already at that time I knew that I was probably missing beautiful experiences that every child has in his or her childhood. But I believed that it would all pass quickly and that it was only a temporary situation. In the depths of my soul I lived a life that was full of activity and content, and I was forever escaping into a magical world of imagination and dreams, where everything was possible.

All of a sudden, with no prior warning, I had been thrust into a different world, a complete antithesis to the world in which I had lived hereto. I was forced to interact with a large number of unfamiliar children and even with adults I had never met before. Without the benefit of any kind of adaptation process I found myself in the midst of social frameworks that were alien to me. Nonetheless, I quickly discovered that I had the ability to adapt to any changes that came along. So far, experience had taught me that things happen in a random manner and I, and the people I knew, had no control over them. I already knew then that any serious decisions I would have to make, I would make on my own. I was constantly seeking solutions that would enable me to cope with the changing circumstances and I often had to improvise a solution in order to extricate myself from a dangerous situation. I invested much thought in my constant search for solutions to any eventuality.

Aunt Angele was a wonderful woman and I grew very close to her, but I never shared with her any of my deliberations and decisions. Although Aunt Angele was very aware of the risks she was taking by harboring a Jewish child and knew how to be careful, she never managed to understand the complexity of the problems that constantly troubled me. She was blessed with many splendid traits: sensitivity and a generous nature, courage, integrity, an awareness of danger and healthy instincts, but she was never able to translate all of them into a complete picture of the situation. She noticed everything, or almost everything, but she absorbed each detail separately, rather than as a whole. Nevertheless, she knew that in spite of my very delicate situation, I had to attend school as often as possible because this was the natural place for children and any alternative was out of the question. As a devout Christian, she was obliged to fulfill the demands of her religion. Thus, the noble thing she did for me was also in line with her moral worldview. I am certain that for her, the harboring of a Jewish child was the apex of her mission in this world and one that might have prepared her for the next. But still, she didn't understand my overall problems and she wasn't always able to play a full role in the harsh events that took place around us, nor to help me with everything that was happening to me, inside and out.

Three, maybe four times a week including every Sunday, I used to attend church. To the priest, I was a good boy — I was polite and disciplined and was happy to fulfill everything that was required of me — and I liked to go there. The silence that usually infused the church had a genuinely soothing influence on me and I would often go early and be the first to arrive for a service. I would sit on one of the wooden pews and a deep calm would fall upon me. Perhaps it was overwhelming fatigue; a tiredness of the body and of the soul. Between the tall church walls I felt protected and the time I spent there provided me with moments when I could be at one with myself, I could return to my real world, put some distance between me and all the theatrics that were unfolding before my eyes.

It is strange how those pleasant thoughts, such as reuniting with my parents and my uncle and aunt usually occurred in a church, a place where I should have felt bad. The private world that came back to me at those moments was not the world shared by all the people who were part of my day-to-day life. Strange, therefore, that here, in the heart of the Christian world, I would return to being that little Jewish boy, consumed with longing for his parents, for a world that no longer existed and for times that would never return. Within a short while, the priest and his helpers would appear and I would sometimes help them with the preparations for the congregation that arrived soon after. Then, all at once, the fatigue disappeared and I would go back to being Henri, the Belgian Christian boy who lived with Aunt Angele in the nice house in that quiet neighborhood.

During my first few months of attending church I refrained from confessing to the priest. He noticed this and would sometimes make a gentle comment, but I had a problem with the whole concept of confession. To confess to a person I hardly knew seemed illogical to me. Why was he, of all people, the man capable of solving all my problems? However, I thought that the idea to consult with someone wiser, more experienced than myself, might help, even though it was in complete contradiction to my newfound worldview, by which I would rely on no one but myself. I managed for a while to evade the pressure (albeit light) put on me by the priest. One day, I asked Aunt Angele what exactly was done in the course of a confession and what its objective was. She explained to me that Christians confess their sins and the priest helps them to atone for them. I asked her what kind of sins she was referring to, did they concern someone who stole or committed murder? Aunt Angele explained patiently that these were not necessarily serious crimes, but could be acts that were "not nice," such as telling someone a lie or not telling the whole truth or, in a moment of anger, wishing someone ill. She pointed out that it was not necessary to actually do anything bad; it is sufficient for someone to have a wish to do so. I mulled this over but found it hard to justify this custom.

Gentle and moral, Aunt Angele never asked me to go to confession, and I noticed that she herself had a serious issue with this matter. Clearly, she understood that these things did not conform to my being a Jew. How could a Jewish child confess to a priest, and in my situation? Already during my first days in her home, Aunt Angele explained to me that it would be best if I were to behave like an ordinary child in every sense; and she pointed out that this included attending church, as non-attendance would have raised unnecessary speculation and questions. So, I attended church and I even enjoyed it. However, this came with attendance at confession. There was something tempting about the idea of talking about myself, of discussing my innermost secrets with someone. Children talk to their parents about what is happening to them, share with them their thoughts and experiences; these were luxuries that I knew existed, but had not been part of my life for a long time. And now, here was a chance to do just that. I wasn't about to relinquish it.

There was also another issue pertaining to my confession dilemma. During Mass, the priest hands out communion wafers — a kind of small, tasty, flat and starchy white disc that melts in the mouth. Everyone who wants one bends down on one knee and waits for the priest to pick one of these discs up between his fingers and place it on the congregant's outstretched tongue. In principle, you can receive a piece of communion bread only after you've been to confession. In other words, a person who has committed a sin he has not atoned for is not worthy of receiving a communion wafer. Thus, the priest would often comment dryly to one of the children who stuck his tongue out for a wafer that he hadn't confessed yet, that he was a bad boy and that he wasn't to try this evasion tactic again. I understood that I had to confess and so I did.

I entered the confessional, which looked like a large elegant closet, artistically adorned with wood carvings; I bent down on one knee and waited for the priest, who settled in the adjoining cell on the other side of a screen that did not allow us to see each other, to ask me to confess. The priest began with a series of innocent questions and led me slowly to divulge the "bad" things I had done or was planning in my heart to do and hadn't yet gotten around to doing. The priest told me that I had to improve myself and to recite several prayers that I had to learn by heart. Only then would I be "pure" enough to be worthy of receiving a communion wafer. Since the priest took an interest in me and my activities, I often took advantage of my situation.

"Father," as I referred to him, "I prayed for something to happen to Roland, for example that he'll break a leg."

"Why did this thought go through your mind?" the priest asked. "He's a good boy, after all. And you're a good boy, too. It really doesn't suit you to think of doing such horrible things. What's happened between you?"

"I collect pieces of shrapnel," I told the priest, "and I think he's stolen a few of them from me."

"You are accusing him of a wicked act," he pontificated out loud, "and you are not even sure of his guilt. This in itself is not a good thing. But you pray in your heart that something awful will happen to him, which is already a crime you are obliged to atone for. Go back to the bench and repeat the '*Ave Maria*' and then the '*Pater Noster*' prayers five times."

I knew very well that the priest would never ask my friend Roland about the theft, but I felt that if I wanted to appear more reliable I had to invent some realistic events from among our experiences. And thus, I found myself telling him detailed stories of things that never really happened. Of course, I couldn't tell him that I was a Jew in hiding, masquerading as a Christian Belgian boy, and that my connection with the church was aimed only at reinforcing my false identity. In fact, what I did was deceive the priest, but it was for a very good cause and my conscience didn't torture me over it. The priest was quite old, he was a pleasant, humane and patient man and I had no intention of making a fool of him. Nevertheless, that was how things developed and he was "taken advantage of" by me in order for me to survive. It was as simple as that.

Later, I often thought that quite a few good and dear people had been "victims" of my ploys in those years. They treated me naturally and openly and gave their best to the boy who was masquerading as someone else. On more than one occasion, those same good and naïve people saved my life and had not even been aware of the lofty act they had committed. Of course, I never exploited them in order to extract any undue benefits from them, but this, in itself, was a kind of deceit.

One of the congregants in the church was a lady who sometimes took a pew next to me. Her son was a member of the group of Flemish children we fought against. She was a very elegant woman, even quite vain, and she usually wore a black frock, with a collar and cuffs that were trimmed with white lace. This dress gave the lady an aristocratic appearance, like that of the female images depicted in the paintings of seventeenth-century Flemish artists. Her face was beautiful, if at times somber. I don't remember her name and don't know if I ever actually knew it. For some reason it seemed to me that she was fond of me.

As well as her son, whom I knew from our "battleground," she also had a daughter, who occasionally came with her to church. I never knew the daughter's name and she, too, seemed to have come out of that same Flemish painting. It was hard not to look at her as her face was the image of purity. Her skin was very pale, almost white, her chestnut colored hair was long and curly and she always wore a white dress. She always kept her eyes lowered when she passed between the rows of church pews and a light blush would rise to her cheeks. She must have been aware of the fact that all eyes were turned on her. She always sat beside her mother as if hoping to hide. I don't think I ever heard her voice although I saw her dozens of times.

Her mother would turn to me with a smile and often said in her warm, deep and velvety voice, "You look like angels. all you choir members, with your ceremonial dress and pure voices. You contribute so much to the spiritual atmosphere in this church. It is mainly because of you that I come to this church." At such moments I was beside myself with joy and felt as if I were floating between dream and reality. How lovely it would have been if I were a real angel and how easy it could all have been. But it was quite the opposite. Those were moments of extreme danger. It would have been most natural in those moments to drop my guard, relax and feel at ease. The warmth that woman lavished on me along with her enchanting pleasantness were very dangerous and I often had to struggle with myself in order to avoid being drawn into committing a foolish act, such as giving away some true detail about myself. There were several occasions on which I was almost unable to contain myself. I used to daydream that she was my mother coming to take me home.

One day, I almost slipped up, so strong was the sudden urge to tell her the truth about who I was and what I was doing in that church, to divulge that my real world was somewhere else and so different. I felt that at any minute I would open my mouth, that my strength was slipping, cracking and crumbling away. And then, with a gigantic struggle, I stood up and ran for my life without saying a word, without acknowledging her, with no prior warning, just like that. Several adults and children in the church noticed my sudden escape. Could I have behaved any differently? I wasn't, after all, in a state in which I could think before taking action. I hadn't considered the repercussions of my behavior. It was a rash response that taught me an important lesson for the future. It was as if I had arisen from a deep slumber. It all took place with such totally unnecessary urgency, but I must have been deeply troubled at the time. My escape from a state of weakness was instinctive and therefore unexpected and of course unconsidered.

After leaving the church so shamefully, I continued to run for as long as I could so as not to remember what had happened. I would have breathed more easily had I only been able to erase this event from my life story. But such occurrences are not erased at the drop of a hat. The run helped me to regain my composure a little. After arriving home, I rushed to my room and closed the door behind me. Aunt Angele must have understood that I wished to be alone. I started to relive the events and came to the conclusion that it wasn't as bad as it seemed although, I had indeed acted foolishly. For a moment I started to believe in the good-heartedness of people and my imagination carried me away to far-off regions and almost drove me out of my mind. That lady, whom I had become so fond of, who looked at me with a lovely, gentle, maternal look in her eye, almost broke into tiny pieces the armor I had built for myself. The sudden need to reveal my true identity served me as a warning. Once again, I was forced to gather my wits and reinstate the defensive shield I had built for myself. My inner strength seemed to have been somewhat destabilized and I had to restore my self-control.

This event left its mark on me. The warning light that it switched on somewhere deep in my awareness continued to burn endlessly. From that moment on, I became more involved with myself than ever before; I shut away all my feelings and desires safely behind a heavy lock and no longer released the various quirks that had hereto made my life more pleasant. I understood that my strong wish to adopt that lady as my mother and my powerful urge to reveal to her my secret took place in a moment of weakness that could have cost me dearly. From then on, I imposed a regime of constant self-control. Besides the immediate lesson I learned with an instinctive speed, I was forced to think up an excuse for my frantic flight from the church. I was aware of the fact that I was actually fleeing from myself, but of course no one else would understand that, not even Aunt Angele. Still, there was no doubt in my mind that my behavior needed explaining. I don't remember the excuse that I made up at the time, when my friends asked why I had made such a hasty retreat from the church, but I felt they were satisfied with my reasoning and no one mentioned the affair again. As for the lady, here the situation was rather more sensitive, but ultimately everything went back to normal. I assumed that my friends had told her the "excuse" I had supplied them with and this seemed to satisfy her. Or, perhaps, she had felt it was better to just leave me alone. In any case, she continued to be nice to me and I remained polite and even pleasant toward her, but nothing more.

I never told Aunt Angele about the incident. Our relationship was very good and our day-to-day routine ran smoothly. I believe she was very fond of me and very concerned about me, albeit in her own way. She expressed her concern in actions rather than words. Aunt Angele was a good and very strong woman and this was what mattered most at that time. In those days, the combination of those two traits was invaluable and often rescued the situation. She had a presence of mind that amazed me. Outwardly, she was always charming, with a kind of earthy, straight-to-the-point charm that enabled people to approach her and feel at ease in her presence. She loved to joke and had her own unique, unsophisticated, down-to-earth but genuine farmer's sense of humor. Even people she didn't particularly like would be given the same simple and direct, warm-hearted treatment as everyone else. No one could tell what was happening inside her head or her heart. She used to say, like her fellow Belgians say in their juicy accent, "*Allez, Allez,*" by which she meant, "Come on; you're not really trying pull one over me, are you?" and a broad smile would immediately spread over the face of whoever was with her. This cleverly relieved her of the need to supply a response to any vaguely embarrassing question that came her way. On several occasions, she managed to escape from a complex situation that could have put her and me at risk.

One of those occasions involved a man who was known for his Nazi sympathies. He lived in our neighborhood and was pointedly avoided by his neighbors. I remember him still. He was a short, blond, ruddy-faced man, with a very narrow moustache that looked as if a line had been drawn above his upper lip. He appeared cold, stern, even frightening. One evening, he turned up at our house; I believe it was in the winter. Aunt Angele and I had agreed between us that if something like this were to happen, I was to run and hide in the place we had dug at the back of the garden. It was very cold. Apparently the man had indeed come to ask some questions about me; and it happened a few months after my arrival in the neighborhood. Aunt Angele invited him in, offered him something to drink and addressed him pleasantly, but was obliged to respond to the embarrassing questions the man asked her. He, of course, asked where I was at this time of the evening and she told him that I was visiting some friends in Brussels and would be returning later. Next, the man embarked on a detailed interrogation: How could she explain the fact that a boy, of whom no one had known anything about, had appeared in her home one fine day. The question was crude in its simplicity and directness, and there was no way to evade it; the response to it had to be convincing in content, but also in the way it was presented. Its tone, too, had to win him over.

Later, when Aunt Angele recounted the incident to me, she admitted that she had been extremely anxious and that the conversation had been within a hair's breadth of ending in catastrophe. At that crucial moment, she'd had to muster all her mental powers and there is no doubt that she passed the test with very high marks. She described to the man the tragedy that had befallen her family when my mother (who, in accordance with the story we had prepared, had been a relative of hers, maybe even her sister) and father had been killed in a bomb attack on Namur, leaving me, a seven-year-old boy, orphaned and alone. As she subsequently recalled to me, she described the event in a way that touched the heart of this stern man, even asking him gently to spare her the pain of elaborating on the subject. Then, in her typically sincere way, she went on asking questions about himself and his family. She even joked with him and thus captured his heart completely.

Actually, Aunt Angele would have been perfectly within her rights to tell the man that it was none of his business. She could even have been angered by his "impertinence," but such a response would have been construed as a declaration of war. She, therefore, quickly weighed her options and concluded that it would be better to be neighborly and welcome him into her home and to reassure him that nothing untoward was taking place there, because this man could have turned out to be extremely dangerous. Later, she was relieved to add that throughout the incident she had been afraid of the dreadful weather that might have forced me out of the hole in the garden.

The man's visit had been sudden and I hadn't had enough time to throw on warm clothes, so that I ran to the hiding place dressed only in light indoor clothing. For more than two hours I had sat there like that in the shelter. Had I come into the house while he was still there, he would certainly have asked me embarrassing questions about my appearance and clothing and I don't know if I would have found the right responses for him. Also, my French was still quite stilted at the time and if I'd uttered a word with my Austrian accent, the man would have suspected me of being Jewish and the whole incident might have ended quite differently. That time, I got away by the skin of my teeth, but that collaborator did not leave us alone, and once every few weeks, he would set up an ambush outside our home.

Several months after the man's first visit, he stopped me on my way home. I was with one of my friends from the group of kids who fought against the Flemish children. We were just coming back from one of those fights and we were dirty and disheveled, and it was obvious that we had been scrapping in the fields. In a tone that was not particularly pleasant, he asked me how I was. His face was rigid; he really was a frightening man. I especially remember his cold, deeply piercing eyes scrutinizing me suspiciously. It was not a pleasant experience. The man asked me what I was up to as well as some other questions that I couldn't quite understand about my past, my family history and myself. I decided, in a split second, to extract myself from the need to respond, as if I was under interrogation, by resorting to a trick often used by street urchins — laughter. In response to the question on what I was doing I burst out laughing. I looked at my friend and repeated the question, "He's asking me what I've been up to," and we both burst out laughing. And, as I pretended to try to overcome my laughter, I told him that we had been bad boys. And again, I laughed. I don't really remember the rest of the conversation but I think he also smiled in response to our impishness and, a few moments later, let us go on our way.

Those were the trying moments that I was endlessly preparing for. In those moments, I made sure to maintain my emotional powers, the source of my self-control and presence of mind that I presented outwardly. Because of moments like these I did not allow myself to relax in the presence of the charming lady whom I had met at the church and who might even have been prepared to adopt me a little. In order to cope with such situations, I never allowed myself to relax and remained alert most of the time. It is for this reason, too, that I never saw Aunt Angele as a full confidante and didn't consult with her.

My friend couldn't stop laughing. For a long time he continued to laugh and joke over the weird meeting with that stern and frightening man, until we parted and each of us went on his way. The whole neighborhood was familiar with the man and he was hated by most of its inhabitants. I laughed with my friend and that, I thought, was the end of the matter, as far as he was concerned at least. But it wasn't quite like that where I was concerned. At that time, I had placed all my resources behind my acting talent and my self-control. But by the time I arrived home, I was seething. Together with the enormous relief, I also felt a powerful surge of emotion and I decided I had to tell Aunt Angele what had happened. She was frightened by what she heard and that same evening we spent a long time planning how we would handle similar events in the future.

The encounter with this man, a Nazi collaborator, left its mark on me. Following every subsequent meeting of this kind, I would isolate myself and conduct a kind of stock-take of the situation. I built a picture, a form of control board with countless small red lights: the state of my identity, my relations with the environment, Aunt Angele's situation, my options for taking action — a crowded picture full of tiny details. After completing the picture, I did my best to ensure that nothing was missing and moved to the next stage — the analytic stage. With a cold and sharp metaphorical scalpel, I analyzed for myself each and every detail in order to evaluate the advantages, the risks and what was required of me. Only after all this, did I prepare myself for various eventualities and unpredictable situations. Often, I had to introduce changes in one or another of the details that didn't conform to my needs or demands. Where language was concerned, I already felt much more confident in my ability, a fact that I found seriously comforting. Being a child, I was unaware of course that my evaluation of the situation was quite superficial, but this was definitely the thought process I developed and nurtured intuitively, an almost animal-like survival instinct. Still, even though I was constantly examining myself, sometimes events were beyond my capabilities to maintain self-control.

Despite all the dispassionate steps I took, I also experienced moments of paralyzing fear. During the bombings I knew no fear as this is an experience that many people go through together. The noise is horrendous and there is plenty of "action" — people run in various directions; one person helps the person next to him and another runs for his life; there is no time for thoughts or analyses; everything happens in a flash. It is different in encounters of the kind I described. It's a different situation altogether. Here, it's a real test, an effort that demands gigantic mental powers, concentration, focus on the person facing you and an attempt to understand at every given moment how he perceives you. You are required to analyze in real time every word that comes out of his mouth, while simultaneously ensuring that every word of yours conforms to the story you have devised for yourself. And no less important than what is being said are the words that are not being said. Is he hiding something? Has my act convinced him?

In the instance I have just described, were my facial expressions appropriate to the tactics of laughter and mischief that I had used? Or, did he sense that my laughter was somewhat false, forced and bogus? It's a struggle of one against another, a real confrontation, with no noise, commotion or unrest. It is a test of mental power, strong nerves, acting talent, language fluency and negotiation, facial expressions and body language, and it all has to appear absolutely natural and convincing. It is a difficult contest, based on accuracy in evaluation, on the senses, on thought particles flashing through your brain. It is a titanic struggle that focuses on minute points of time and place. There is nowhere to hide; everything is open and exposed. Had I not taken all these things into account, I would have lost the campaign. Every such defeat could have cost me my life and maybe even the lives of others. I had no doubt that in this matter I had only myself to rely on. In such cases, the tests were difficult in the extreme. I understood that I had no safety net and that if I fell, I fell.

The hiding place we built at the back of Aunt Angele's garden was meant for times when it was better for me not to be seen. There weren't many such occasions, but I think there were some when it helped to alleviate some danger and maybe even to save my life. Aunt's Angele's eighteen-year-old son, René, was the first to have the idea of building the shelter, shortly after I arrived at their home. René was very tall and quiet, but with a sense of humor. He was a little coarse to my liking, at least at the start of my stay with them. Until then, I had had no experience in social intercourse with unfamiliar people and he frightened me a little and I decided I had to be careful around him. However, I was soon able to understand his unique personality and I became very fond of him. All of a sudden, I had obtained a surrogate older brother. Unfortunately, he later disappeared for a long time.

René suggested digging a pit at the bottom of the garden and camouflaging it so it would blend in with the rest of the flora behind the house. We immediately set about the job of digging. We worked quickly, knowing that a sudden visit by an unexpected guest was liable to expose our secret. We dug energetically, covered it all with branches and the hiding place disappeared among the garden's dense undergrowth. The camouflage was perfect. I could hide there and no one would suspect a thing. The hiding place could not, of course, withstand the test of a dog, but here I have to fast forward a little and mention an important detail that can be quite flattering to some of the people in Aunt Angele's neighborhood.

Many years after the war, I learned that several other Jewish children had been hiding in various places in the neighborhood, although, to this day, I don't know who they were. In any case, the knowledge that more Jewish children were living in the vicinity explains, in retrospect, a painful event that gave us a good number of sleepless nights.

One fine day, a car appeared on our street with two or three German soldiers, accompanied by an officer. The car moved along slowly and it was obvious that the soldiers were surveying the neighborhood. I was at school at the time and Aunt Angele wasn't at home, but we learned about it from a neighbor who mentioned it nonchalantly. From the tone of her voice, it was obvious that the neighbor had no suspicion that a Jewish boy was hiding in the area. Aunt Angele's response to this new type of rumor was not exceptional, although she decided that we take quick and intelligent action. She was worried that the Germans would return to the area. No one could guess what the reason was for these reconnaissance patrols, but we immediately considered the worst and thought together about the steps we should take. Actually, there was nothing wrong with our official cover story: My parents had been killed in a bomb attack on Namur. Aunt Angele, a relative, had decided to adopt me in this difficult period and to give me a loving home and, especially, the opportunity to lead a life that was more or less appropriate for a boy of my age.

Aunt Angele didn't know how I would behave if confronted and she was also a little worried about my Austrian accent. Although I had already lived in her house for a year and spoke French almost like a Belgian boy, she felt that my German was better and was worried that I might blurt out a word in German in the course of a conversation with German soldiers, which immediately would have given me away. Aunt Angele reckoned that someone in the neighborhood had reported to the authorities that a Jew was hiding in her home. One way or another, she decided that we must make every effort to prevent a meeting between the Germans and me.

The evenings became a problem, when we had to switch on the lights. It was not customary in our neighborhood to close the shutters in the living room, only in the bedrooms. Aunt Angele feared that closed shutters would arouse suspicion. The house we lived in was part of a long row of semi-detached, two-story buildings. The living room was always on the ground floor, which made it possible to look in through the front windows and see me. Aunt Angele decided that with sundown, I should go to my hiding place at the bottom of the garden and await developments. And then, later in the evening, after receiving an "all clear" signal, I could go back to my room on the first floor and go to sleep in my soft bed. The main thing was not to be seen in the living room and not to be around if the Germans were to knock suddenly on the front door.

There was another problem: In order to avoid an encounter with Germans, I was obliged to miss school, and this happened quite often, even for long periods. For some reason, I wasn't so worried about missing school, but I missed the neighborhood "wars" between the Flemish and Walloon kids and also the church and all my activities there. Excuses had to be found for all these absences, and I had to invent reasons that were acceptable not only to my friends but also to their parents. During the day, I would sit at home, hiding behind the curtains. The moment I noticed a German soldier in our vicinity, I would run to the garden and take shelter in my hiding place until the danger had passed. Most times, these turned out to be false alarms, but I could never let my guard down. In the evening, as soon as it became dark, I would slip out of the house and make my way to the hiding place and wait.

Sometimes it was dark in the dugout. There was a smell of mould in the air and during the winter months it was freezing cold. Usually, the time I spent there was quite brief, but sometimes, when the fears were greater, it could last for many hours. At those times, I knew in advance that I was in for a lengthy stay and I prepared myself with blankets and food, but often I was obliged to run there in fright at the last moment. At times such as those, the dugout became the safest place for me. It was my stronghold, and no one else besides me stepped into it. Inside the dugout, the earth was muddy, so we covered it with tiny branches that soaked up the rainwater after a downpour. These little branches also helped warm my feet a little. We lay two bricks on the ground, with another brick across them for me to sit on.

Despite the harsh circumstances, I loved that dugout. It was mine and only mine. No one but me sat in it. Notwithstanding the cold and

The house in which I hid in the suburb of Kapelleveld, Brussels.
The small window in the centre was my bedroom in which I spent hours
feeling happiness, fear and anger.

damp, I felt a kind of security there and the warmth of home. For me, it symbolized my life. It wasn't just another hole in the ground that we'd dug and fixed for a long stay under extremely basic conditions. It was my own private, warm nest. Inside it I could sit quietly, stretch myself out, create for myself a whole new world and feel that no one else could ever reach me. When the wait was extended, I would sometimes raise the lid of twigs and leaves in order to look around me. In daytime, I could look at the plants in the garden. There were redcurrant bushes and other fruit trees whose names I have forgotten. On the other hand, I well remember the vegetable patch. Aunt Angele grew the vegetables we ate for supper. I also spent many hours studying the sky. Different images spread themselves out in front of my eyes, changing shape in unison with the moving clouds covering the Belgian skies during most of the seasons of the year. At night, the scenery took on completely different features. Then, the trees and shrubs metamorphosed into statues and enriched the entire stage with a look that was mysterious and threatening. When the wind blew, the trees began to waver, all too often challenging my peace of mind. There were moments when I felt a fear that frequently turned into real terror, especially when I allowed my imagination to run wild. Sometimes I would forget that I was in hiding in Aunt Angele's garden and I imagined I was in the heart of an African jungle.

The isolation and distance I felt in those long hours in the dugout intensified the feeling of distance between me and the house and I started to envision myself all alone in an unfamiliar place. It was then that I was at the height of an adventure, in a fantasy world, in some prehistoric cave somewhere between heaven and earth. Often, I would turn on my daydreaming mechanism that led me to unlikely provinces. When the weather was pleasant and caressing, I spent long periods daydreaming and I would find myself in a world that was beautiful and green, warm and friendly. The people there were pleasant and very soon, my loved ones would appear — my parents, Hanna'le and Salo. The frightening dugout turned into a house of dreams. In my imagination I extended the size of the place, padded it out, added lighting that created warm corners, in the center of which I would sit with the people I wanted to have with me during those moments and hold lively conversations with them all, following the stage instructions of my own devising.

I was the producer, director, stage manager and leading actor. Sometimes, I would exchange roles. In this imaginary world I often included the garden shrubs and trees around me. I gave them life: Every statuesque bush was given a role and had a place in the grand production of my creation. The stage I created was always warm and very colorful. The actors smiled and always looked at me with benevolent expressions. Often, I was sorry when summoned to come out of hiding. I would erase in an instant the pleasant world I had created in the dugout and make my way back to my dull and threatening routine.

My hiding place was located about 20 meters from the living room in which Aunt Angele sat and about 30 meters from the street. I was very close to any commotion, to anything that could happen outside the dugout. Despite my daydreaming, I often felt terribly lonely during those moments, but not because of the distance. Even in the huge African jungle it is possible to connect with a familiar place that has life in it, it is possible to encounter some person, perhaps an animal or some godforsaken villagers living in isolated mud huts; hence, you don't feel so solitary even if you've never been to that place. And yet, there, in a place with which I was quite familiar, only a few meters away from people I knew, I could feel such a cosmic loneliness that spread throughout my whole being. My brain experienced so much turmoil. When I felt that dreadful fear, I immediately tried to recover and find a suitable remedy for it, which was when I created those delightful moments of assembling my loved ones and it was they who reinstated my sanity.

One evening, someone knocked at the door. It was quite late and I was already asleep in my room. According to the script we had outlined for ourselves, there should have been the noise of an approaching car, followed by screeching brakes, or the sound of an engine being switched off, but on this occurrence there was nothing. Alarmed, Aunt Angele came into my room and forced me to run to my hiding place in my pajamas, as she shouted to the people outside that she was putting on some clothes and coming to open the door. She pulled herself together, quickly tidied my bed and went downstairs. When she opened the door she found herself facing two or three soldiers together with an officer. The following morning she told me the rest.

Aunt Angele's behavior towards the visitors was most courteous, but utterly devoid of cordiality. According to her, she displayed no sign of fear or trepidation. She conversed with them calmly, self-confidently, knowing that she must not arouse in them any opposition that could be disadvantageous to her. She remained perfectly calm and collected. The reason for the visit, according to the officer, was that information had reached their office about the presence of people in the vicinity who hadn't been seen there before. I believe there was also mention of children, but I am not sure about this. Aunt Angele asked them to come in and sit down. She told me that they had behaved politely, but she had been subjected to a fierce interrogation and had had to contend with several trick questions. Since she had assumed at an early stage of the interrogation that someone had reported me and that in fact the Germans knew about the presence of a child in the house, she decided to take a preventive route. She explained to them that so many family tragedies had taken place in Belgium and probably in other countries, too, that the structure of many families had undergone considerable change. As an example, she described our own family and told them about me, adding that it was a pity that I wasn't there at the moment, because otherwise they could have seen for themselves how families were reorganizing themselves and relatives were ready and willing to provide each other with a helping hand, especially when a child was involved. She even had the audacity to invite them to visit again "when the boy is at home." This all took place with exquisite courtesy, but as I have said, with no demonstration of cordiality or sympathy. They asked her how many rooms there were in the house and Aunt Angele went so far with her audaciousness that she even showed them the garden in which I was hiding. They took a few steps into the garden and about two or three meters before reaching the dugout, Aunt Angele turned on her heels and marched briskly back to the house, the German soldiers following her automatically.

After the Germans had left, Aunt Angele didn't come to fetch me and I understood that she was afraid they might return suddenly, or worse, that they were keeping us under surveillance. It was clear to me that I would have to spend the rest of the night in the dugout, which wasn't particularly hard and I wasn't afraid. The only thing that concerned me was the fact that I didn't know what was happening, what had been said, why it had all taken place and how the sudden visit had come to an end. I only knew that they had left and that in itself was quite good and important. At daybreak, Aunt Angele approached the dugout and told me in a whisper to run to my room. I obeyed the order happily but wasn't able to run because my legs were practically paralyzed from crouching uncomfortably for so many hours. I was probably also frozen, since it was winter and the cold outside was fierce. The walk from the dugout to the house lasted forever.

When I got to my room, Aunt Angele was already waiting for me. She was very upset and hugged me tightly. She was a strong woman and unused to emotional outbreaks, but it seems that the intensity of the experience had shocked her and knocked down the wall of self-control that she had built around herself and had become part of her personality. I hugged her back quite hesitantly and with a little force, which gave way to some vague embarrassment on my part, too. Aunt Angele was a restrained woman and I had adopted this trait. I therefore found this break in convention highly embarrassing, even if it brought me a little joy. I had begun to feel a fondness for Aunt Angele, but I made great efforts not to like her too much. I decided to reserve my love for my mother and father — in absolute secrecy, of course — and I interpreted any expression of my sympathy or love towards Aunt Angele or anyone else as a betrayal to my parents.

Aunt Angele realized that she had been through a crucial test in the management of my future and hers, at least for the upcoming period. She had a good feeling and she reckoned she had acted well and quite wisely. But, as happens in such cases, we couldn't know how the Germans saw the matter. She repeatedly asked herself out loud if she had said the right things: Had she behaved appropriately? Was the measure of normality she had tried to exhibit fitting to a situation of that kind, not too little, not too much? After all, in such situations, it is the tiniest nuances that play such an essential role and we had no way of knowing if she had passed the test. From that moment on, I was able to discern a hint of anxiety on her face that never disappeared until the war was over.

From the very beginning, she had known the dangers involved in hiding a Jewish child and she was prepared for it. She had arranged all the necessary tools for coping with the situation and we had even synchronized our cover story, our life stories and the relationship between us. This was the correct thing to do, since we had to be ready for all eventualities. However, the situation changed at that moment, once we had been put to a real test. Until that evening, everything had been going according to plan and had worked perfectly in our day-to-day routine. Aunt Angele was careful, maintaining her presence of mind when she encountered German soldiers or when obliged to evade a neighbor's embarrassing questions. Her success until then in stepping between the raindrops greatly increased her self-confidence.

The stories we had prepared and coordinated as to my presence in this place had become an inseparable part of her life and she almost believed that it was entirely true. The stories we had composed sounded even more true and feasible than reality itself. We had managed to build a life story and a list of adventures that could fit into any situation, except that we were living at a time in which everything had changed. Lives had dissolved and collapsed and people were forced to undergo fundamental changes. Everyone was wary of everyone else; people were all somewhat suspicious of each other. People spoke less. There were people who were ashamed of their actions and kept their silence. On the other hand, there were also people who did good deeds, which sometimes saved lives or assisted the allied forces, but they were unable to talk about them to anyone. They all kept quiet. It was a time for acts, not for words, not for boasting. There were a lot of people who took advantage of entire families who had also been forced to leave their loved ones.

When the Germans had entered Aunt Angele's home and presented her with questions, for which every answer required gargantuan mental powers, she had suddenly felt that her world — and mine, too — was about to collapse at any moment. However, since she had prepared for just such a moment, she was able to control her emotions. Her composure and her talent for acting appeared to have persuaded the Germans that she was telling them the truth. But she herself had been through a terrible trauma, the effects of which stayed with her until the end of the war. For the first time in her life she felt an overwhelming fear, a fear that penetrated to the very depths of her body and soul. Expressions of this terror emerged only the next morning, after we met and hugged. She looked broken and very pale and I started to worry that she might die. Soon after, she went to bed, her body trembling all over and she asked that I leave her be. She only ordered me not to leave the house and not to open the door to anyone.

Over the following few days, Aunt Angele spent most of her time in her room. She almost didn't leave her bed and didn't function. When anyone rang the doorbell in the evening, a neighbor or a friend of Aunt Angele's, she would get out of bed, put on a dressing gown and go downstairs to open the door. If, by chance, I wasn't already in the dugout, I would make my way straight to it, settle myself in and wait for the danger to pass. This was how we lived. It was a nerve-wracking time.

Since Aunt Angele had decided that I wouldn't go to school for a while, "so as to allow us to see how things developed," I was unable to go to church and was forbidden to join the activities of my friends, the Walloon youngsters. Most of the time, I was forced to stay at home, hiding, terrified of a sudden visit by the Germans. It was an unusual situation, quite absurd really: A nine-year-old child being obliged to manage the entire household was a rather heavy responsibility. For several days, I had to go out to buy bread and other items of food, which I did with great vigilance. I would run and leap and as soon as I saw anyone from afar, I would slip into a doorway or hide in some garden before continuing on my way. After Aunt Angele recovered and was able to get out of bed, she forbade me to go out and it was she who did the shopping. I don't remember how long I stayed at home, but the Germans did not return and after a while, I went back to my routine activity.

Aunt Angele, notwithstanding her emotional steadfastness, found it hard to recover from the ordeal. Although she functioned properly and fulfilled her day-to-day tasks in the best way possible, she was no longer the same strong, confident woman who loved to joke and didn't feel pathetic. She became a worrier, more careful and also more suspicious. She explained something to me that I had already known for a long time: People couldn't be trusted and it's every man for himself. Some years after the war, out of her love for humanity and her desire to help the underprivileged, she joined the Jehovah's Witnesses. Aunt Angele believed in people and her mission was to help them live decent lives, before finally arriving in paradise.

At that time, I asked myself what would have happened if the Germans had come back to our home shortly after that incident. I was disappointed with Aunt Angele, since I had no doubt that she would have completely fallen apart and this suddenly changed my attitude towards her. I felt I could no longer rely on her and I started to regret the fact that I was staying with her and having to listen to her and to follow her instructions as my parents had directed me when they made me swear I would be a "good boy." Since that was my understanding at the time, I realized that I was in real danger, as she was, too, and I soon understood that I had only myself to lean on. I remember my hesitations as I tried to think of someone who could advise me, but there was no one in my vicinity whom I trusted and could help me consider my situation and the options at my disposal. I had no way of knowing if my plan was practical. All the friends I could think of were out of the question and their parents were not reliable enough in my eyes. For a brief moment I gambled on the priest I used to confess to and I nearly put the idea into action. For several days, I planned my fateful sentence: "Father, I am a Jew and I am in danger. I have a plan that I have been thinking about in case the Germans should discover my real identity. I would like to consult with you because there is no one else except you who can help me. You are a man of religion, a holy man and I know you won't betray me."

As I sat in the confessional, the sentence stood on the tip of my tongue and I was just about to set it free, when, at the last moment I was able to find the strength to overcome that powerful urge to share my troubles with others, and instantly fell silent. Instead, I did something unspeakable: Without waiting for the priest's blessing that is given at the end of the confession, accepting the prayers that are supposed to condone me for my sins, or asking for permission to leave, I slipped out of the confessional and ran home. Again, I lost my cool; once again, I got into unnecessary trouble; and again, I would have to invent an excuse for my strange behavior. I felt that I had behaved in a childish manner and I had to compensate for it.

All that evening, I sat alone in my room, deep in thought. Again, I had succumbed to a moment of weakness, of self-pity for being alone in the world with no help or support. I felt that familiar physical pain gripping me that almost caused me to collapse. I recovered after a while and tried, once again, to analyze the situation logically. I repeated to myself that I was alone in the world and had to protect myself from such mistakes and, especially, to stop trying to find help. The next day, I went to apologize to the priest with some story or other. At first, he appeared angry, but I knew that he would forgive me in the end because deep in my heart I felt he was very fond of me.

I didn't tell Aunt Angele anything of this. Also, I managed to plan my getaway if the Germans ever returned to the house. I reckoned on several possibilities, based on several potential circumstances. I have forgotten the details of my plan, but I remember being determined to disappear and to try to survive on my own. The only part of the plan of which I can remember a little was to get out of Brussels one way or another and to make my way to a village, where I would lie in watch over several houses and choose one where a childless couple lived. I would have told them my standard story of losing my parents in a bomb attack and then offer them my help doing any work available. Once I had decided what needed to be done, a profound calm fell over me and my strength was restored. Fortunately, my feeling of weakness soon disappeared, too. I felt strong again, with a good measure of self-control. In an instance, I dropped my futile attempts to find someone to support me, I mustered myself anew and, suddenly, I felt wonderful.

It was at about this time that my arm, which I had broken prior to the war, started to trouble me. I had no idea as to the kind of surgery I had undergone after breaking it and knew only that the fracture had been complex and had required three or four operations. However, the pain started about a year after I arrived at Aunt Angele's and the use of my arm became increasingly restricted. It transpired that in the last operation I had had a metal pin inserted into my elbow, which had started to rust. This led to an infection that was the cause of the pain I was suffering. I don't remember how all the treatment started, but I suddenly found myself in some hospital and the doctors decided that I had to undergo further surgery as soon as possible.

The operation was not pleasant and it raised quite a few fears, especially due to the hospital's registration process and also because I was in the hands of people about whom I knew nothing. Of course, the fact that I was circumcised did nothing to alleviate the fear of my true identity being discovered. Aunt Angele was worried that I might have hallucinations during or after the operation that would give me away or that I would revert to speaking German when under general anesthesia. They were still using chloroform to put patients under, which is something I remember with horror. Every attempt to anesthetize me was accompanied by a genuine battle. The doctors and nurses were obliged to hold me down firmly because I had no intention of falling asleep by means of that dreadful drug, until I could no longer resist and I gave in and went under. I was terribly sick when I awoke and it took a long time for the nausea to dissipate.

To this day, the smell of the chloroform and my attempts to fight the medical team awaken unpleasant memories in me. But, ultimately, I got through the operation. I stayed in hospital for a few days and I remember being constantly alert, ready for any eventuality, with Aunt Angele's visits being the only pleasant moments during my stay there. Back home, I had to stop all strenuous activity for a month. My arm was then more or less back to normal and, like the time before, I found special ways to use my arm as much as possible and to overcome the handicap that still bothered me.

All too often we were obliged to witness — and often to be victims of — bombings by the Allied forces. These bombings were especially harsh on the civilian population. On the one hand, we were happy to see airplanes belonging to friendly forces, but then we learned that their hits were not always accurate and sometimes caused terrible destruction and loss of lives. Admittedly, people could take shelter in any of the air raid shelters that existed throughout the city, but they weren't always able to make it there in time. I remember one such heavy bombing that occurred whilst Aunt Angele and I were in the town center. All I can remember after the air attack is destruction. Many people had been hurt, which exacerbated the game of "Russian roulette" that had become an integral part of our lives in those days. At any time, we could have been the next victims, but strangely enough, it was a feeling that didn't especially disturb us. People became conditioned to living with this threat and were more occupied with their daily routines than with the danger that lurked from above. An encounter with German soldiers was a much more frightening prospect than "friendly fire."

On several occasions, Aunt Angele and I were outside when the sirens went off. At those moments, I felt that there was something hypnotic in their terrible screaming sound, because at that very moment, it's every man for himself and he knows that within a very short time, his fate will be sealed. The experience is of titanic dimension and there is an awareness of the enormity of it. Most of the people were very restrained, sometimes daring to display a vague, wan smile, but most definitely maintaining their composure. There was a concept of appropriate behavior. People avoided creating a commotion. Everyone dealt with the situation in his or her own way, but held on to their respectable mien. It was obvious that some people were unable to overcome the terrible situation that gripped them, although neighbors tried their best to be supportive of one another and offered each other their help when they could.

We, older children, took a lot on ourselves; although it might be more correct to say that we took our lives into our own hands. I noticed the concern this aroused in the hearts of the mothers, who tried unsuccessfully to keep their children nearby. Some of the children, me among them, seemed to anticipate with baited breath the longed-for moment when the planes arrived. To us, the approach of the "friendly" planes symbolized hope and communication with the outside world, the world that would come to rescue us from the occupation; this knowledge gave us renewed power. It was like a brook from which we could all drink our fill. We saw in it the beginning of our salvation, and it was not only the children who felt this way. The adults, too, looked up to the skies with an expression of awe and yearning and a prayer that all this would soon be over. The roar of the approaching planes was pleasant to our ears but as soon as the bombing began, the yearning and hope were erased from people's faces, to be replaced by worry and fear.

The adults mainly ran for shelter, as did some of the children — those who were forced to stay with their parents or, in most cases, their mothers. As for us, the neighborhood "ruffians" (of whom I was one), we always managed to slip away from the adults and wander through the streets while the bombs, shells and shrapnel fell. We assumed they came from the anti-aircraft artillery spread about in the vicinity of our school. It was then that the real party began, taking the form of a giant competition over the collection of pieces of shells and shrapnel that had landed over a large area. In the midst of the commotion caused by the falling bombs and the terrifying noise that could be heard throughout the whole area, we would break into an insane sprint. Nothing could stop us from carrying out the mission. We were gripped with a sense of madness and only when the planes had disappeared did we calm down and rejoin the adults.

I should point out that I don't remember any of the kids who ran amok in the streets ever being killed, but each time, after this kind of thing happened, Aunt Angele used to scold me. People were killed in the bombings, but none of the boys in our gang of "shrapnel collectors" was. Apart from our mutual desire to win the competition, it was impossible not to be captivated by the fascinating magic of the streets under a bomb attack, which were, of course, empty of people. Those pretty, quiet, friendly streets had turned into a neighborhood of ghosts; it was quite a frightening, surrealistic sight when all around there were the constant echoes of what sounded like powerful thunder storms. After it was all over, we would return home with our loot, feeling a genuine source of pride. Those were powerful moments and I remember them well, because under those circumstances I became a free boy. That wildness filled me with the vitality and energy so necessary for my continued existence.

One day, a man who bore a remarkable resemblance to my Uncle Salo turned down one of the streets near our house while I was on my way home from school with a group of friends. Perhaps I just imagined seeing him, but so strong was the belief that the man I had seen in the street was Salo that I was convinced it really had been him. It could not have been otherwise. I was shocked and found myself being drawn to him. I made up some excuse to be rid of my friends who were surprised by my impulsive and sudden decision to desert them; I acted out of an uncontrollable urge and did not hold myself accountable for the repercussions of my actions. The person who was walking slowly along the streets of my neighborhood had me hypnotized. I couldn't let go of the image, so I followed it. After about 15 minutes I saw the man enter one of the houses in the neighborhood. He was perfectly relaxed and behaved naturally and I assumed that he must live there. Through the white curtain that covered the large window I was able to see him moving around in the large living room.

I stood in front of the house for about two hours. Pictures of Salo and Hanna'le came back to me one after the other and I remembered the days when they would sit and play with me. Suddenly, I felt a terrible pain at the thought that those days, which seemed to belong to another world, had gone, never to return. The pictures flickered quickly in front of my eyes, like a silent movie in which I was also one of the actors. During the hours that I waited there, I even felt sorry for myself for a moment, but above all, this event aroused a powerful yearning in me. I continued to stand in front of the man's house and lost the strength to pull myself away. I had suddenly been thrown back into the warm bosom of my family that had been lost to me for so long. Although I understood that it was not a good idea to stand in the same place for such a long time, my legs refused to budge. All I needed was to attract attention to myself for the neighbors to inform the police that a boy had been loitering near their house for hours. I knew I was behaving in an entirely illogical way, in complete contrast to all the decisions and rules of behavior I had set for myself, but my legs wouldn't move. They remained nailed to the pavement, heavy, as in a dream. With all my strength I wanted to pull myself away, but I simply couldn't.

Suddenly, a boy who appeared a few years older than me, came out of the house. He looked at me but continued on his way. He took a few more steps and turned back to see if I was still there and finally disappeared. I used all my self-control not to go and ring the bell and to ask once and for all if that man was indeed my Uncle Salo. In my heart I knew that it was someone else and eventually, I was able to move away from the spot. Sad and agitated I returned home. I refused any food Aunt Angele offered me and didn't want to talk to her. Instead, I closeted myself in my room and spent the night in the company of my parents and uncles. The following morning, Aunt Angele told me that I had spoken a lot during the night in a loud voice and she appeared worried. I told her nothing of what had happened the day before. The following evening, I returned to the man's house, and again, I waited. I think I knew what I was waiting for and how I expected this affair to develop. The house appeared to have turned for me into a focus of yearnings that I had no control over. The yearnings intensified with my feeling of loss and the depression and agony that accompanied them, but they also allowed me sometimes to "go back home" and that was a good thing. I went back there every evening for several days.

One evening, when I was leaning against the fence that surrounded the house, the man came out, approached me and asked why I had been standing there for several days watching his house. At that moment, a woman appeared at the front door, probably his wife. The man spoke to me in a soft voice, with great kindness. He seemed curious and there wasn't as much as a hint of suspicion or anger in his voice. The woman smiled at me. They asked if I was interested in coming into their house and I accepted their invitation happily. Their son, who was sitting in the living room, raised his head for a second; he looked at me and returned to the picture book he was holding in his hand.

I had mixed feelings: shame and disorientation vis-à-vis warmth and happiness. In fact, I didn't know what to say to them. I hadn't planned this possibility. Indeed, there was a slight resemblance between the man and my Uncle Salo, but no more than that. I felt I had made a fool of myself. It was something that could have developed into a serious and dangerous situation. Everything I had built up with so much effort — a new identity, image and behavior that was appropriate for my age — could have all gone down the drain. The man had short and curly hair, similar to Salo's, and his gait really did resemble my uncle's. The two strangers were most cordial and invited me to sit down. I was deep in contemplation. At that moment, I understood that the vague resemblance between the two men had returned me to a previous world with such force as to create in me a dangerous confusion between imagination and reality.

Now I was facing a problem that was not at all simple. How was I to get out of this complicated situation I had got myself into? I continued to say nothing. Very gradually, I began to regain control of myself and was more aware of the circumstances in which I was caught. In an attempt to appear at ease and to impart a feeling that I wasn't remotely embarrassed, I started to smile even though I was still trying to find a suitable excuse for being there. In the end, my hosts were the ones who managed to extract me from the mental stagnation I was in.

"You look familiar," the woman said to me. "You probably live in the area, don't you?" I nodded. "I think we've seen you in church," she added. "I sing in the choir," I said with some pride, and felt myself gradually getting back on track. Immediately, I felt I was divesting myself of my stress and decided to tell them something that was close to the truth and acceptable to grownups. "I am Aunt Angele's nephew. My mother and father were killed in an air raid a year ago and I was miraculously saved. When my aunt learned that I was still alive she decided immediately to take me to live with her and for the time being she is taking care of me. I have no brothers or sisters."

My story had an obvious and shocking effect on them and I decided to tie the rest of it to this tragic event. "A few days ago I saw a man who looked remarkably like my father. And from that moment, I have been behaving rather like a baby. I followed him; to be more accurate, I stalked him. I tried to prevent him from noticing me because I didn't want this magic to end." I felt the tremor in my voice intensify but had no control over it and went on, "You must understand. I suddenly saw my father and it all came back. You are the man who looks so much like my father. I couldn't tear myself away, so I stood for hours beside this house and I didn't have the strength to leave and go back to my own home, to reality. I knew you were not my father, but still I wanted for this 'magic' to continue. And then you saw me and here I am. I am ashamed of my behavior and beg your forgiveness if I have caused you any discomfort."

The emotional monologue hit the spot and I managed to shed genuine tears. At that moment, I understood that I had succeeded in getting myself safely out of that highly embarrassing situation. Those two good people, who had listened to me in silence, were clearly upset by my story and started to treat me gently and sympathetically. I understood that I had succeeded in my mission, but now I was facing a rather difficult problem that had to be solved with some urgency. It was obvious that I had to sever myself quickly, before any emotional relationship developed between us. Their congeniality quite scared me. I also noticed that their son, who was probably an only child, didn't seem too pleased with his parents' enthusiasm. He was watching me with demonstrable indifference. My impression was that I wasn't to his liking and I had to avoid arousing his envy or any other feelings that could harm me in the future. The boy was a problem. Maybe he thought I was about to rob him of his parents. He had heard the whole story and showed no sympathy. On the contrary, seeing his parents' warm response towards me, he obviously saw me as a dangerous rival; all of a sudden an orphan boy turns up in his home and now he's about to assume a central place in his parents' hearts.

I decided to take my leave of them. I thanked them for the kindness they had shown me and their understanding, despite my inappropriate behavior. I stressed the urge that had taken control of me and caused me to behave secretively, like a thief in the night. I noticed that the couple was very touched by the whole incident. It had been easy enough for me to make those claims because they were a real part of my life. It was how I really felt and a testimony that it was the "devil" that had possessed me and given me no peace. The hours I spent laying in wait beside their home was additional proof. I had indeed become possessed by some kind of "madness"; unless it could have been just a weakness of mind. The vague similarity between the two men had driven me slightly insane and as a result of this passing madness I had been given a chance to spend some time with my uncle. I had tried to maintain a grip on this illusion with every fiber of my soul, until I was "caught in the act." I subsequently met that charming couple several times, but each time, I tried to shirk them off, after just a brief conversation. After all, I wasn't in a position to develop a relationship with them, which could have turned out disadvantageous for me. However, I got quite caught up in this episode while it was taking place and continued to deal with it even after it ended.

This might have been the toughest of episodes that I was involved in, because I had been drawn into it to a point that was hard to withdraw from, but it wasn't the only one. Often, I would scrutinize people, completely anonymous people, and search for any similarities they may have to my dear ones. I would build an entire movie script around their personality, but it was all in my mind and it was impossible for anyone to discern what was taking place. I breathed new life into them, imagined a different environment for them and gave them an identity of my choosing. Thus, in the depths of my imagination and under surreal circumstances, I connected once again with the people who were dear to me. I had no control over these feelings, but they gave me renewed strength to move on with my life.

During those years, the conditions I lived under squeezed out most of my energy. Even with my parents, I don't remember ever having laughed heartily. This doesn't mean I didn't have fun with them, that there were no occasions we enjoyed together, but everything was always in a rush, always in an attempt to catch a moment of happiness, of laughter, with the knowledge that it could all change in the blink of an eye. We were unable to relax for even a moment, to let go, to relieve some of the tension. Anxiety accompanied everything we did, even on the Sabbath. My parents were observant Jews and I used to go with my father to a very small synagogue, where people prayed with passion and an intensity of a kind I do not remember from other times in my life. I saw men begging God to help them alleviate their suffering. Some of the men entered a whirlwind of movement, their bodies swaying and their heads jolting uncontrollably. There was a great deal of power in this, which impressed me very much. I think my father was a little different. His voice was not heard and his movement remained very restrained. He remained withdrawn and introverted. I was unable, as a child, to understand the power in his introversion and sublime restraint. However, with the passage of time, when I reconstructed those moments, I understood that my father's pleas were no less intense than of those enthusiastic pleaders who had me hypnotized with the passion of their prayers. For those persecuted people, these were brief moments of grace.

There were periods when my father did not go to the synagogue, because it would have involved too much danger. On those occasions we would spend the entire Sabbath at home. The atmosphere was wonderful because we were together, but fear and uncertainty were always hovering in the air; no one had the strength or the will to laugh wholeheartedly or tell jokes. Admittedly, there were times when we laughed at something we'd heard or seen. The laughter would relate to a specific quote or a particular event, but it didn't have the power to break the barrier of anxiety, that was constantly present among us. Sadness dominated everybody. People looked depressed. Their concern stared out of their eyes, but I don't recall seeing desperation. Our daily struggle for survival did not allow for such a "luxury."

People were too busy surviving, and first and foremost, they worried about their families. The order of the day was to find food, sleeping quarters and decent shelter for such a time as their circumstances would deteriorate. My parents, my uncles and the few Jews I visited with my parents appeared to be busy all the time, concerned with securing their exhausting day-to-day existence.

Things changed for me when I came to live with Aunt Angele, but as far as I was concerned, it had become worse. At first, I did not have the willpower to laugh or to rejoice as ordinary children did. Only later did I discover those rolling, uncontrollable, uninhibited outbursts of laughter; the kind of laughter that comes out of the very depths of the soul, that is real and liberated; a *joie de vivre* that takes nothing into account, that takes itself to the very end. I saw that most of the kids in the Flemish and Walloon gangs I played with were like this. They were happy, despite the difficult times we lived in. As soon as I had befriended them and had become one of their group, I, too, burst out laughing, just like them; but my laughter was momentary, an immediate reaction to something that had happened and not an expression of my real feelings.

Basically, I felt bad. My sadness was constant and not a fleeting event, as with my friends. I was fighting for my life and my sanity, especially after I had gradually begun to understand that my parents were in the hands of the Germans. I wasn't in my natural environment, nor with the people I loved. On the contrary, all those people whom I loved were far away and I couldn't be sure that I would ever see them again. Additionally, I was undergoing a process of self-education and establishing a new identity, in an attempt to put down roots in a place that was utterly foreign to me. I was so busy with all these concerns that I had no time left to account for what I was feeling. So, I think I smiled a lot. A smile on one's lips broadcasts ease, contentment, peace of mind, equanimity — all the facial expressions that I wished to impart to my surroundings in order to conceal my real mood, which was grim. I was sure that I had developed the necessary tools and acting ability that would be of great help to me in the future. To this day, I am aware of other people's body language and often observe them as if in a mirror reflecting emotional expressions of happiness or suffering. It is a tendency I have taken with me since the war and from which I am unable to free myself.

Since Aunt Angele lived in quite a pastoral area, I could hear the twitter of birds and listen to the sounds of nature. Time stood still during the days when I hid in the dugout at the bottom of the garden, my senses became honed and I was able to listen to every sound that nature provided. The silence that surrounded me was my only interlocutor and it was with it that I created a relationship and had my first romance. Oddly enough, when the worst scenario was threateningly close, I felt a kind of peacefulness, but also a dreadful weariness. It was a time when I was able to live with little food, to make do with very few comforts, without all the luxuries that make our lives so pleasant. Closeness to nature and the sense of security provided by my hideout often brought a tiny smile to my lips. Such was the feeling of protection I had in its vicinity that I was filled with real joy. Nature embraced me and enveloped me in a swathe of magic. I was enchanted; I was in seventh heaven. The smile on my face was testimony to this.

I arrived at Aunt Angele's home in March 1943. At first, my parents would visit me from time to time but they stopped coming after three or four months. I was very angry with them. I thought that they had forgotten about me, that they were more comfortable without me, and I developed all kinds of explanations for their disappearance. Initially, I asked Aunt Angele why my parents had stopped visiting me so abruptly. She tried every possible way to explain that since their visits had also placed me in danger, they probably preferred to refrain from coming too often. There were also various other explanations. In defending my parents, Aunt Angele was unable to conceal a hint of embarrassment that I couldn't help but notice. By 1942, the Germans had already intensified their anti-Jewish manhunts, to which I was often witness. Thus, by gradually delving deeper into this sensitive and highly charged issue, I was able to persuade myself that it was impossible for my parents to have suddenly forgotten me or had decided to distance themselves from me, until I eventually reached the unavoidable conclusion that they had been captured by the Germans. I understood instinctively that they would not be visiting me for a long time, at least until the war was over.

From that moment, my state of mind changed and I became a rather unapproachable, introverted and quite sullen boy. I continued with my normal routine but the abyss that had formed within me now kept me locked behind a strong wall of loneliness and desperation. I had seen quite a few dead people by then, mostly as a result of bombings and air raids. I knew that Hanna'le and Salo had long been in the hands of the Germans. I thought about them a lot and missed them, but this was the first time I was actually thinking about their death. It wasn't death as a general, probably natural phenomenon, but Death with a face. As soon as I realized that my parents were in the hands of the Germans, I took into account that they were liable to die.

My attitude to death was completely naïve. No one had ever talked to me about it, even when I had seen dead people. Death had become a part of my life, causing me to grow up in an instant. No longer was I able to separate day-to-day experience from the end of life, which meant death.

From now on, the two concepts were inextricably intertwined. I looked around me and saw the same people I had seen before, but something about them had changed. More accurately, it seemed that something in me had changed. Until that moment, I had seen the same people as they were – alive, active and reacting. Now my viewpoint had changed. From now on they were no longer the familiar images from everyday reality and I started to imagine them dead. I went so far into the realms of my imagination that every single person whom I observed or conversed with died a different kind of death. That is, everyone, with the exception of Aunt Angele. I refused to imagine her dead. I was absolutely unable to resign myself to the fact that she, too, was mortal. She was the source of my security, the ultimate security wall. Nor did I think of my parents in terms of death. I couldn't imagine them without life, but cold logic told me that they were most probably in real danger. An intense fatigue came over me as a reaction to harsh changes; a feeling of emptiness that I had already felt several times before – a kind of lack of purpose to my struggle. If my parents had been captured, it would have been reasonable to assume that I, too, would not manage to escape, and if that was the case, what was the point? These reflections plagued me from time to time and weighed very heavily on my moods.

At that time, my nocturnal brain appears to have been unusually active. The main motif in my dreams was a powerful desire to chase Germans and punish them. The chase turned into an obsession and these dreams did much to improve my spirits. Naturally, I dreamed them at night, but there were also many dreams that filled my days whose format was quite different. My daydreams were based on a pattern that was wholly the fruit of my desires, the fruit of a determined decision. Their outline was chosen carefully and all the rest was created by a wild imagination. This combination allowed me at any given moment to respond, to beat and to avenge myself on anyone I wanted, whenever I wanted.

On the other hand, awakening from the dreams I dreamed at night was always accompanied by pain as I hoped to change things, to have some influence. It all appeared so real and promising, but here it was, only a dream and again I awoke to my futility. I realized that there was nothing I could do to change the situation, except in my dreams. The spiritual uplift and feelings of power I experienced in my dreams made way for emptiness and loneliness. But my thirst for revenge never left me. Every time I encountered a German or a number of German soldiers, or even someone who was known as a German sympathizer, I would activate this mechanism — here I am hitting him, insulting him or even worse. And so I developed a kind of double life for myself. My life was quite miserable, one in which I was inevitably the victim, the pathetic, defeated character, but then, after I activated this special mechanism of mine, I was the hero, the victor who always had the upper hand. This ability gave me a great deal of strength.

For quite a long time, the Germans had placed a battery of anti-aircraft guns next to my school. There was much Allied bombing at that time and I suppose the Germans' decision to place the battery at that spot was connected to that. I was going to school fairly regularly then and my friends and I used to walk past the soldiers stationed nearby. They were usually seated on the hill, fooling around. Sometimes, they would wave at us in greeting. My friends didn't dare look them in the eye, because of the instructions they had been given at home. "If you encounter a German soldier, don't look him in the eye, because you can never know what he's up to," was what parents told their children.

I, on the other hand, would look straight at them. Of course, deep inside, I was terrified, but I had some inner urge to do so, despite the danger. As I looked at them, I was able to remember what some of them looked like and as soon as I was alone in a safe place, at home for example, I would shout at them, beat them and even kill them with my fists, all of them, one by one, down to the very last man. Then, when I walked past them again the following morning and they waved hello to us, I would give them a victorious smile, because as far as I was concerned they no longer existed. What the others saw was no more than an illusion; only I knew the truth. The hatred lurking within me must have been so strong as to put me in danger, but, fortunately, my imaginative mechanism, which allowed me to cope with the aggressive outbursts I was subject to, seemed to have saved me more than once from unnecessary complications.

One day, my friends and I went to play football in a large field not far from our school. We were quite a large group and it was afternoon, right after we'd finished school for the day and we decided to play for about an hour before going home for lunch. We marked out a pitch and goal posts, organized the players into teams and started to play. We must have been making quite a lot of noise, because five or six young German soldiers from the anti-aircraft battery suddenly appeared and started walking towards us. At first, we continued to play, but when they stood around the pitch and started cheering us on and clapping their hands, they looked like a bunch of youngsters looking for some fun and some of the boys, quite naturally, waved to them and invited them to join the game. Obviously, the Belgian kids didn't like the Germans either, but these soldiers looked merry and quite innocent. There was good chemistry between the two groups, although, because of the language barrier, there was no possibility of exchanging a word with them.

I was the only one there who understood German, but none of my friends knew my secret. My French was still not fluent, as would be expected from a boy who was born in Namur, an important city in the Walloon area of Belgium, where French was the spoken language.

I suppose that my accent in French tended more to Flemish, but I didn't know Flemish. I knew that I couldn't behave differently from all the others and that I was expected to be nice to the Germans, like everyone else. I also couldn't allow myself to stand out from among the children who were quite enthusiastic about the idea of playing with those soldiers. For kids our age it was quite a compliment to be able to play against nineteen- or twenty-year-olds. The soldiers were happy to accept our invitation to play and came onto the marked-out pitch. Each of them cordially shook hands with us, then divided themselves between the two teams and we started to play. Naturally, the game changed. We barely made it to the ball, but I saw that my friends were amused by the soldiers' achievements, which provided them with some impressive goals and were even proud of them.

I was in quite a quandary. The Germans appeared more like a bunch of guys who were out for a good time rather than on the hunt for Jews, but there was no knowing what would have happened if they had realized that they were playing with a Jewish kid. I continued to play like everyone else and tried to keep a low profile — not to play too well or too badly; to laugh like the others — no more, no less; to behave naturally towards them, but also with a certain respect, as any child would behave towards an older person who was stronger and more skilled than him; and to keep to the middle road and not to deviate. I was a juggler walking on a high tightrope for whom any slip could end in tragedy. When a soldier smiled at me, I smiled back and if he ignored me, I ignored him in return. It was the behavior of a chameleon, adapting itself to the complicated situation. The trouble was that I couldn't even retire from the game because then I would have attracted attention to myself, which would have required an explanation to my friends, and the Germans might have detected my Austrian accent. So, I giggled and smiled but tried to avoid any conversation that might have revealed my mother tongue and arouse the suspicion of the Germans and may even have caused my friends to wonder why the Germans were commenting on my accent. My friends had obviously become accustomed to my accent and asked no questions.

We were all tired and sweaty after the game and we lolled about on the grass to rest. I sat with all the others, pretending to relax but I was far from calm. I was tense, anxious and very aware of every move the Germans made and the possibility that, for me, this strange situation could end in a death sentence. The entire sequence of events flashed through my mind at a dizzying speed and I realized that I had no control over the situation; I could have done nothing else. It was a kind of decree that actually leaves one with no option to initiate or fight. It wasn't I who caused it; it was pure chance. I was very worried and very sure that the only thing I did have control over was my own behavior.

I thought to myself: What would I do if one of my friends were to suddenly ask me something then laugh at me and the others suddenly joined in? I thought that in such a case, it would be best to join in with the general foolishness and joke along with the others, but I knew that I lacked the suitable background. My history in the neighborhood was extremely short and not even very transparent — my accent was different and I didn't really belong. So, I lay on the grass pretending to be quite tired and started talking to one of my friends who was lying next to me. It was clear to me that any silence on my part would arouse more suspicion than a superficial conversation with one of my friends. The Germans laughed, spoke loudly and said it had been such fun because it reminded them of home. Then, one of the soldiers, who seemed to have a more senior rank, told his mates that they should be getting back to work. The obedient soldiers stood up and, before leaving, said to us in German that they hoped to have a chance soon to play with us again. They waved goodbye and went off. Luckily, nothing had happened, everyone had had a great time, but for me it had been a difficult experience and one that drew from me a great deal of emotional strength.

My behavior, which resembled that of an ordinary child living in a family environment with parents and the addition of several siblings, together with my rigorous church activity, was of course just a figment of the truth. Admittedly, for a child of eight or nine, my personality was fairly robust and well formed, but I was constantly aware of the fact that my entire world was one of lies, from beginning to end, consisting of fabrications, misrepresentations and a false identity on which my feverish imagination fed itself.

This duality became routine to me; nonetheless, I sometimes felt a powerful urge to just be myself. At such times, I would closet myself in my room for a whole day without emerging even once; I didn't go to school and didn't go downstairs to eat. Aunt Angele knew that I wasn't to be disturbed. She knew, most probably instinctively as we had never spoken about it, that for me, this day was something sacred, something that belonged to me exclusively and there was no space in it for anyone else. During the months we had been living together, Aunt Angele had managed to get to know me very well. Already a day or two before I locked my bedroom door behind me, she was able to sense that a change in my mood was about to take place. She used to wait for me to go downstairs to eat in the dining room and then she would serve me a good, lovingly prepared meal. She never asked me any questions about my seclusion.

I don't know if those were moments of crisis in which I suddenly felt the need for self-pity. Or maybe I succumbed to overwhelming fatigue and needed a day of rest to rehabilitate myself, before moving on. Or, perhaps, this was my only way to cope with the situation. I don't know which of these possibilities was the true case, but as time passes, the greater is my tendency to believe that this was my way of rehabilitating my existence, each time anew. In this way, I connected to my roots, laid my weapon in the wardrobe and stood alone in the room, unmasked, exposed and alone with myself. It was my own private sanctuary and anyone who tried to enter it would be desecrating the place. Here in this place, where I had succeeded in cleansing myself of all ugliness and corruption, I was reunited with my parents. We would embrace each other. Sometimes, I would try to consult with them and those realistic figures filled the room. I talked to them out loud, tried to hold onto them, to blend into them, to feel their touch, and I would spend the day in this manner. I even allowed myself to weep, until the yearnings became too intense. Then, I felt it was time for me to stop. I felt that if I continued like this I would be liable to cause myself harm and destroy the defensive wall I had worked so hard to build for myself. Then, the day came to an end.

The return to full activity after a day of isolation was slow and gradual. I felt that such a day of communion always provided me with a great deal of strength and vitality, especially in the long term. It was a day of divine joy tempered by sadness but its uniqueness laid in the purity that subsequently filled every cell in my body and soul. It was this that I wanted. And it is for this reason that I didn't allow anyone, not even the good, gracious Aunt Angele, to participate in this ritual of convergence. The sphere of my communion with my loved ones was devoid of all contamination, from any hint of the evil routine of my day-to-day life; I didn't establish a shrine or a stage to my parents, I tried only to reconstruct our tiny nest, which consisted wholly of warmth and love, a nest that we had somehow managed to sustain at the beginning of the war. There was no room there for anyone else apart from us. I bore this experience in my heart for a long time after I left my bedroom.

Today, too, as an adult, I don't share my memories of my parents with other people. Of course, my parents were not granted a grave; I say no prayers for them in public and I don't pray out loud. This private and intimate experience is all my own and I share it only with my parents. I have succeeded in preserving the purity of this relationship to this day. The feelings sometimes awaken when I am attending the synagogue or visiting the cemetery, but not necessarily; sometimes they awaken at moments and under circumstances that are completely unexpected and then I "commune" with them and my memories. There is no extra space in this triangle of my mother, my father and me. A picture of the three of us has been carved in my memory ever since our last meeting.

The meetings with my parents were conducted under conditions of extreme secrecy. They would come to Aunt Angele's home about twice a month. I remember clearly how I used to reproach them at those meetings with harsh criticism; they had, after all, promised to visit me at least once a week, and they weren't fulfilling their promise. I was angry with them and I proved to them that I was right. They tried to gently explain to me, each time they came, that they were unable to visit me more frequently because that would be putting me in great danger, but it was all to no avail. When the visit was over, we used to go out. My parents walked together and I walked alone behind them so that no one would realize the connection between us. Of course, they would have preferred — for everyone's safety — to leave the house on their own and walk along the country road up to the tram station, which was next to the girls' school. But I wouldn't agree to that and insisted on accompanying them until just before they boarded the tram. At one of the dark entrances to the school, we spent a few minutes together and said our goodbyes once again. Then, they would continue on, board their tram and I would return to Aunt Angele's house. Actually, I would not do so immediately. After our leave-taking, I would go back, stand behind a tree with a thick trunk that grew at the entrance to the girls' school and watch as they boarded the tram. Only after the tram pulled out did I leave the spot.

The last time I saw them we did exactly the same, except that on that occasion my complaints must have been especially fierce and we stood for quite a long time beside a side entrance to the school. I remember how confused my father was by my complaints, and that he continuously tried to appease me until he had run out of words. My mother burst into tears, and then I felt a terrible regret and understood that I had behaved very foolishly. A child, it would seem, can be extremely selfish. We then hugged and kissed with an intensity that was greater than ever before, unless this is just the way I remember it. But, to this day, I can still taste the power of this separation that turned out to have been our last goodbye.

Did my parents sense anything? Did they know anything? I can't say. Years later, I learned from Mr. Hourmont that my parents had been denounced to the Germans by a Jewish man or woman.[10] My mother had told him this. My parents were arrested a few days after our last meeting. In a letter to my grandmother and her son (my Uncle Avshalom) in Israel after the war, Mr. Hourmont wrote that he had done everything in his power to persuade my parents to

---

10   After many Jews went into hiding, the Germans employed informers to point them out on the city streets. One of these, a Brussels Jew known as Jacques, was particularly successful in this unsavory work.

The side gate of the school where I used to meet secretly with my
parents and the place where I last saw them.

escape from Brussels and seek a hiding place elsewhere, at least for
a while, but in vain. They were caught just a few days after their last
visit to me. I don't know for certain what the reason was for their
decision to remain in their house and conduct their lives as usual, as
emerged from Mr. Hourmont's letter. Still, I do have the idea that
my parents simply refused to continue running. They were tired of a
life that lacked all meaning; they felt hurt, despised and must have
decided that there was no point going on in this way, especially now
that they had succeeded in "ridding themselves" of the one thing that
was dearest to them — their only son — for whom they had found a
safe haven. From that moment — this is what I feel in the very depth

of my heart — they entrusted their lives to fate and maintained their self-respect to the end.

One day during the war, I don't remember the exact date, more German forces arrived in our neighborhood. We discovered this when we came out of school and noticed that they were focusing all their activity on the nearby anti-aircraft battery. We were a bunch of kids and we stopped to have a look at what was happening. There were several trucks and armored cars and, it seemed, several additional anti-aircraft guns. All of a sudden, new soldiers appeared, in addition to those who were stationed there permanently. It was obvious to us that something unusual was about to happen.

We witnessed a lively movement of troops, busy unloading freight and erecting small reconnaissance and other spacious tents. I especially remember the voices. Orders were being issued, always in loud voices, firm orders that offered no question, argument or appeal. They were all very energetic young soldiers, working confidently, with each of them knowing exactly what he had to do. They reminded my friends and me of a line of worker ants. After a while, the soldiers noticed us and signaled to us to clear off. We responded at once and made our way home. I told Aunt Angele what we'd seen and she decided to go there and see with her own eyes what kind of change had taken place in the German Army's deployment in the neighborhood. I watched her from the window, talking with the neighbors.

This sudden fuss raised questions among the local inhabitants, who weren't particularly keen on the goings-on around that anti-aircraft battery. When she returned, Aunt Angele announced that I would have to stay at home for the next few days and would not be attending school until we knew what was happening. She also stressed that I was to cease immediately all my activities with my "fighting" friends as well as in the church. In the evening, I went to my hiding place in order to prepare it for a stay, which, this time, could turn out to be a lengthy one. I spread out several blankets, brought in a little food and some water. At least I had time to prepare the place in advance instead of having to do a panic-stricken sprint to the bottom of the garden with no chance of collecting things for an extended stay, as had happened on several previous occasions. The following morning, two or three of my friends decided to visit me and rang our doorbell. I ran to the dugout at the bottom of the garden and Aunt Angele opened the door for them. She told them I had been called away for a few days to the city of Namur; this was one of the regular excuses for my absences.

During the days that followed, soldiers started patrolling the neighborhood streets. Their behavior was polite and agreeable and did not arouse any animosity. It looked as if they were walking around aimlessly, whiling away the time. However, at least according to Aunt Angele, the increased German presence in the neighborhood aroused the suspicions of the inhabitants and caused them to spend more time closeted in their homes. I spent entire days indoors and during some of the evenings I sat in my dugout, as it was imperative for me to avoid being seen through the front window when it was dark outside and the lights were on inside. The problem then arose with regard to my absence, since no one knew how long the Germans would remain in the neighborhood. Two or three days later, the neighbors began saying that the Germans had carried out some kind of maneuver and had fired several artillery shells. Some even said that the Germans had reinforced the anti-aircraft battery following information received regarding heavy allied bombing, which had increased recently. There was much tension in the neighborhood; those simple people felt as if they had become the very epicenter of the war and that, of all places, it was where they lived that the most decisive events were taking place.

At the same time, there started to appear in the Belgian skies German rockets that whizzed by and exploded in more distant locations. We were told that those rockets were aimed at England, but some of them fell not very far from where we were. The first to appear were the V-1 rockets[11] that made an irritatingly dull,

---

11   Having first developed the V-1 flying bomb (also known as the buzz bomb or doodlebug), the Germans advanced to the more lethal V-2 rocket. Beginning in September 1944, over 3000 V-2s were launched by the Germans from launching pads located in northern France against Allied targets, mostly in London and later in Antwerp and Liège, as well as key sites in the Netherlands.

monotonous, unthreatening kind of buzzing sound as they flew overhead; a sound like that of a transformer, with an hypnotic, somewhat calming element to it. When a V-1 appeared above us it was hard to disconnect our glance from it. Unlike the Allied bombers, which we regarded with love, despite the terrible destruction they sowed, every time a V-1 appeared the people's expressions would change instantly to animosity, anger and revulsion.

In actual fact, these rockets caused less damage than those of the Allied Forces, since their hits were more accurate and did not leave behind widespread destruction. But, still they fell and exploded and even injured quite a few people. The moment the familiar buzz sounded, the concern became palpable; we were scared of the bomb falling nearby, or even directly on us. This fear related to something specific, something that could be defined. We could point at the source of the danger, that single element which was passing over our heads. This is why everybody was standing in the street, tensely following the rocket's route, until the engine's noise disappeared. This was the moment of stress, when I often thought people had, quite simply, stopped breathing; the look in their eyes was frozen, their mouths hung open, their bodies turned to stone. They all became statues, not a sound was heard, and even nature was silent. This tableau continued for no more than a few seconds but seemed like an eternity. At the moment of explosion, everyone breathed in relief. People made their way to the spot where the bomb fell to examine the damage and to offer help if necessary.

Sometime later, another kind of rocket started to appear in the sky: the V-2 — a new rocket that was more frightening and left us with utter uncertainty. The V-2 made no sound and the silence aroused in everyone a frisson of fear, but with it there was also a kind of reconciliation: Whatever has to happen will happen. It transpired that the new rocket had replaced the V-1 and we started to miss the old one. At least this was what the adults were saying, in jest of course. The presence of these rockets weighed heavily on the residents and was the main topic of conversation at that time. I don't know if there was a direct connection between the dispatch of those rockets and the reinforcement of German troops in our neighborhood, but the camp was dismantled shortly afterwards, leaving only the soldiers involved with the anti-aircraft battery next to the school. The additional soldiers disappeared and I was able to resume a more or less normal routine.

I don't remember if, at that time, Aunt Angele knew anything about my parents' fate. If she didn't know, she must surely have guessed what had happened to them, but chose to say nothing. She exhibited a great deal of sensitivity towards my situation and did her best to alleviate my anxiety during those days. I realized quite quickly that something serious had happened and assumed that they had been caught. I don't remember discussing it any further, but deep inside I had doubts with regard to the explanations I was hearing. Only in early 1945 did Aunt Angele and I discuss it openly and I expressed the hope that they would return soon.

Throughout this entire period I kept everything secret, in my heart. My feelings moved from profound desperation to great hope and to impatience to know what each day would bring. There was not a day in which I did not think about my parents. Not all day, of course, because I was very involved in my other activities, but thoughts of them never left me. I also gave much consideration to my Aunt Hanna'le and Uncle Salo, who had disappeared a year before. Sometimes I would bring them into my little family unit, too. They were the only people to be thus privileged.

I often felt that I could no longer bear the emotional burden that was running around in my heart and I had the need to share with someone else everything that was happening to me, but as long as the war continued, I kept it all to myself. The object of my confidence at the end of the war was Uncle Francois, Aunt Angele's husband, who was stationed in London. I sent him two postcards that expressed very well what I was going through. The cards were written in 1945, when it was already possible to write freely. The postcards were written in French. If we take into consideration the handwriting, the number of spelling mistakes and the bad grammar, even though I was already ten years old, it is easy enough to notice my inferior French — most likely the unavoidable result of frequent absences from school during the first years of my education.

## First Postcard

> *Dear Uncle Francois,*
> *Thank you very much for the postcard you sent me. I told you that some people have said that my parents had been liberated. I don't know if they are alive or not. I would so wish for them to be still among the living. I hope to see them again as soon as possible as it's been two years since I last saw them.*

## Second Postcard

> *Dear Uncle Francois,*
> *I now hope that my parents have been released, since people are saying that Transports 21 to 26 have been released. My parents were on Transport 21. All this is making me more and more impatient.*

These were the first postcards I sent to Uncle Francois, who returned home shortly afterwards. Clearly such postcards could not have been written and sent during the war, as this would have betrayed my real identity and exposed Aunt Angele and me to immediate danger.

My life changed as soon as I understood that my parents had been captured by the Germans. I was eight years old at the time and it was clear to me that from then on I had only myself to rely on; with the help of Aunt Angele, of course, but her failings forced me to be constantly on my guard. I was alone in the world. I no longer had parents, brothers and sisters I had never had, my dear Uncle Salo and Aunt Hanna'le had already disappeared and I knew nothing about the rest of my family; I didn't know where my grandmother was, I could barely remember the rest of my family and I certainly didn't know where they lived. I found myself alone, with no ties of any kind to the past. The only person I had any faith in was Aunt Angele. I also knew of Mr. Hourmont and remembered him well, but it was clear to me that I must not make any contact with him. I didn't even know if he was still alive. Nor did I have a clue as to exactly how I had come to be living with Aunt Angele. We had never spoken of it, or whether she knew of Mr. Hourmont; I never mentioned him. Everything I know today was told to me after the war.

In the meantime, equipped with my fictitious identity, the details of which I had learned thoroughly and repeated often with the help of Aunt Angele, I set out to confront the reality of my new life. I knew that this false identity was to guarantee my survival until the storm blew over. I was well aware that this was no game and I looked upon it with utmost gravity, understanding that my life depended on it. It was at that stage that I decided to change, to befriend the other neighborhood kids, to attend church and to behave in a manner that conformed to my new identity, the place and the new circumstances of my life. The change I undertook was good for me. I enjoyed it and felt that I really was a different person. The sense of emotional resilience and physical strength indicated my break from the past and entry into a harsh world, but one in which I had some chance of survival. I was involved in the plethora of activities in which most children my age were engaged.

Aunt Angele noticed all these changes. She must have understood that they would be of use to both of us in the event of an occasional hitch, which came all too often. Still, I had a feeling that she sometimes watched me with sadness, because she understood that all I wanted was to deny my past, my parents, my religion and my origins. We never discussed these things, which was for the best. She found it hard to internalize the change I had undergone, which I had ostensibly taken for granted. As an especially conscientious and moral person it was hard for her to reconcile herself to it, but she never said a word. Her sensitivity, gentleness and graciousness were boundless. How strange it was that only after the war did she start to talk to me about my parents.

Somehow I was able, unconsciously, to develop a set of animal-like senses that guided me in this war for survival. When times were bad I would go into hiding and wait for things to improve, but even if times were good, I knew deep down inside me that I was playing a role and that everything I did or showed wasn't genuine. I was a charlatan and although this caused no one any harm, it was charlatanism nonetheless. The children all around me were able to behave in a natural and spontaneous way, whereas I had to consider and plan every single step and to adapt everything to the circumstances. I laughed like all the others, was enthusiastic, but at the time, I was constantly observing myself, weighing every single word; all this demanded that I maintain superhuman self-control. My talks with the priest in the confessional were an exercise in guile. I planned and "fabricated" my sins so they'd sound convincing for a boy of my age; I was unable to liberate my thoughts for even a moment, because it might have led to a catastrophe. I understood this perfectly and acted upon it implicitly. The colossal urge that occasionally awakened within me, such as the time when I very nearly allowed it to drag me to a genuine confession, was clearly a human and natural one.

Life has taught me that the toughest imposters preserve their own small corner of truth, where they are able to identify and examine themselves and which occasionally permits them to return to their own selves. At that time, I was not aware of the importance of this ability to return to one's personal identity if one wished to maintain one's sanity. I remember moments of weakness and a slackening of my nerve, but I didn't allow them to continue and I immediately tensed up. I think I was probably acting naturally but was unaware of doing so. A recharge of the strength I needed always came just in time. Today it seems to have been a miracle.

Relations with Aunt Angele were excellent but as I have already stressed, we never had any real conversations. I never poured my heart out to her. We lived side by side, but there was no intimacy between us, and the moments when I secluded myself in my room to "spend time with my parents" were extremely important to me. Those were the times when I would break down and weep incessantly, when I would unpeel all the layers that covered me, before pulling myself together and moving on. So long as I knew nothing of my parents' fate, I was able to hold onto some kind of hope. At first, they explained to me that my parents couldn't visit me for a while because of the difficult situation and I had no choice but to accept this explanation. However, after a period that seemed to last an eternity, I realized something had happened to them.

Only two years later, at the end of the war, did Aunt Angele tell her friends, in my presence, how grown up I was and how I had managed to cope with the sudden disappearance of my parents. But it was no wonder. Deep down inside I knew that something had happened to them, because there was no other logical reason for their continuing absence. Still, although the truth penetrated my awareness, it was a long time before I actually reconciled myself to it. Inside me a terrible crisis was raging and my success in overcoming it was in spite, or perhaps because of, the days and hours I spent in seclusion. At those times, the hope that they would appear accompanied me throughout the war. The power of that hope was expressed in the two postcards I sent to Uncle Francois at the end of the war. At the time of writing them I was indeed full of a burning hope that I was about to see them very soon. Later, and also even after the war, when my family had contacted me, I wrote to my grandmother and uncle in Israel saying that I was still hoping to see my parents. However, as time went by, this hope became increasingly vague.

Several months after the war's end, when the chaos reigned among the Jews of Europe in their search for surviving relatives, I began to feel the doubts gnawing at my heart and growing increasingly stronger. In Sisyphean attempts to discover what had happened to them, we approached Jewish and other organizations, until it finally became clear that it was all over, and my concept of reality became unfixed. No longer did I nurture unnecessary illusions. The wait for the official confirmation was a nerve-wracking period. It extracted more strength from me than all the evasive tactics that were integral to my life in those years and I was under unbearable stress. I eventually received all the details of my parents' transport. Years later, Mr. Hourmont told me that he, too, had been arrested by the Germans shortly after my parents had been led to the Gestapo offices and he had found himself sharing a cell with them. According to him, my parents were interrogated by the Gestapo. He told me that they were beaten, especially my mother. It was the last time he had seen them. I don't know how Mr. Hourmont had managed to escape and I never asked him.

As for my parents, they were sent immediately to the Malines transit camp in Belgium and from there to Auschwitz. They left

Malines in July 1943, on transport number 21, which consisted of 1,563 people and arrived in Auschwitz on August 2, 1943. Of this number, only 466 people survived the extermination that took place that same day — August 2, 1943. Of the 1,563 people on transport number 21, 40 were still alive after the war. My Uncle Salo and his wife Hanna'le left Malines on August 11, 1942 on transport number 2 and arrived in Auschwitz that same month, together with 999 other people. That day, 477 people died. At the end of the war, three people had survived from their transport. I learned these details some time after the war, possibly from the Red Cross.

With the war over, life took on a new direction.[12] The world around me was immersed in a kind of euphoria that drew everyone in. I was witness to outbursts of joy and emotional expressions of solidarity.

The entrance to the Malines transit camp from where my parents were deported to Auschwitz.

12   Although most of Belgium was liberated in September 1944, the war continued in the Ardennes until January 1945.

Inside the Malines transit camp.

Love flowed from every direction with a force that was electric. After those terrible years that had come to a sudden end, the atmosphere was of absolute madness. Everyone wanted to talk to each other; people hugged one another in the streets like relatives or lovers meeting for the first time after long years of separation. I was not part of this joy.

Naturally, the end of the war was a cause for happiness; I had believed that I would be able to reconnect with my past, which I had almost erased through so much effort. However, behind the hope there lurked a huge darkness and much unrest. I felt as if the security and the seemingly solid framework I had built for myself, here in this quiet Brussels suburb was about to crack and founder and a new kind of terror gradually grew in my heart. What past was I talking about? Where were my parents? Where were Hanna'le and Salo, who disappeared without trace? Although I was an Austrian Jew, I felt wonderful as a Christian Belgian kid, a member of the local church choir, doing a weekly confession for my so-called sins; a member of a Walloon street gang that held fierce battles against the Flemish for reasons that I had no idea about; residing with Aunt Angele to whom I had become accustomed after quite a long time. What now? The only thing that gave me strength was the hope that my parents would return, and maybe even Hanna'le and Salo.

I used to turn up regularly at some office in order to check if any news had come in (could it have been an office belonging to the Red Cross? I don't quite remember). The clerks were nice and never ignored me. They, too, hoped on my behalf. I often waited outside Aunt Angele's front door for the postman to arrive and always went back in empty-handed. I was sure that from now on I could cease playing a role that was not my own, that I could behave like any other kid, that I could stop having to hide, to pretend; but was this what I really wanted? Until that moment, everything had been clear; I knew exactly whose side I was on, how to function, how to behave in any situation. I was a well-oiled machine, with almost no hitches. The situation had been extremely difficult, but one can adjust and can somehow even enjoy it a little. What was to become of me now that the war was over? Where was I in all this? Who was I, damn it? I was alone in the world. Where would I go? Was I supposed to return to the nothingness where my past was hidden? How? With whom? For what?

I was confused. At first, I lost all sense of direction. I couldn't find myself. I didn't know what was going to happen to me, where they would lead me, or who would lead me. And I was afraid of the truth. The hope that my parents were still alive had given me strength and a powerful faith that, in time, had turned into an obsession and given me no rest. But besides that, I had felt a kind of irritating emptiness. Although, until then, my life had been full, there had never been a moment of remission, of quiet, of calm. I had always been as taut as a coiled spring, and even when I was on my own I was troubled by thoughts of my situation. I was constantly engaged in a search for solutions to the worrying phenomena that was taking place around me.

Although the war had ended, I continued to seek ways to improve the outward signs of my identity and I also often thought about the future of my relationship with Aunt Angele. Once in a while, I would recall the (few) people I had known before and were no longer alive. All these things troubled me, aside, of course, from my daily activity, the normal activity of a kid of my age. In the back of my mind I started realizing that from now on, my life would change and that I would need to peel away some of the important layers that had provided my life with a lot of content and security up to then. On the one hand, a sudden emptiness occurred with the knowledge that I would no longer have to struggle; and on the other, a fear of the future filled me with sadness and a sense of having lost my way.

Looking back, it is quite hard for me to reconstruct what I was feeling then, but I do remember well Aunt Angele's concern for my emotional state. This concern was expressed so obviously that I felt obliged to pull myself together and control my behavior so as not to weigh too heavily on her. She was not a woman of words. She didn't try to use sophisticated means to persuade me that "everything would be alright." She simply looked at me with mournful eyes, until I understood that I had to show sympathy to her and start toeing the line in order to alleviate her suffering. I understood she had become very attached to me, but I didn't know it was so strong. For me, too, it was a new situation that I had to cope with. In fact, I had become very attached to her, too. The painful two years we had spent together had made us close. Every event we triumphed over we counted as a victory. Often, we would celebrate this victory — always in a restrained way, with no exaggerated displays of emotion, but with a great sense of relief. Over two years we built for ourselves a framework for day-to-day existence founded on trust and a willingness to sacrifice and in the midst of all these elements, there germinated the seeds of love. This closeness helped me and I made superhuman efforts to function normally despite my quite shaky mental state.

In retrospect, I often thought that the end of the war was the worst time of my life. I found myself in the center of a whirlpool of events and feelings. All around me everyone was feeling joy and spiritual uplift. People were ecstatic, unrestrained, running around from place to place, not knowing where they were going; it was as if they were trying to stop the moment, to prevent it from passing, so the euphoria wouldn't dissolve, anything rather than a return to reality. Everyone lost control completely. They were sick of reigning themselves in, of caution and suspicion. They longed for disorder, for anarchy. Boundaries between what was permitted and what was not became blurred and people were swept away on a huge wave of joy and love. I took no part in it all. Admittedly, I was still quite young (ten years old) and everything that took place around me belonged mainly to the adult world, but this was not the real reason.

Although I felt relieved, because I understood that the hell of war had come to an end, it was also obvious to me that my future was unclear. I knew that a new chapter was about to open in my life, a chapter that didn't appear particularly pleasant, of which more was obscured than revealed. It was the beginning of my encounter with real life, without the support of my dear ones. Deep inside I knew that the moment of truth was approaching and that this, more than anything, was what I feared. During the two years of daily struggle for survival that I had been through, I had been strengthened by hope. Now all that was over and very soon I would know the truth. There was still hope in my heart, except that now it was tempered by concern. The wait for developments was tantamount to awaiting a sentence that would seal my fate. My future appeared vague and threatening.

I started to attend school on a regular basis. I didn't reveal my real identity to my school friends and, as far as they were concerned, I was still the same boy who was absent from school for long periods and was now turning up for all his lessons and to all the neighborhood social events, and was generally behaving like any other neighborhood boy. To my surprise, no one paid attention to the changes in my behavior and we didn't discuss it. Life took on a quiet and rather dull routine. However, things were different with regard to the priest.

One day, shortly after the end of the war, I went for confession, as I had been doing for over two years. Instead of telling the priest about my sins, I told him in a direct and simple manner, which surprised even myself, that I was Jewish, that I had been hiding under an assumed identity and since the danger was over, I could now tell the truth. The priest didn't move, did not reply and did not respond; he was silent. I realized that his shock was no less powerful than my own. But still, I had been active in the church, I had participated in masses several times a week, I had sung in the choir and had often assisted the priest with all kinds of chores in the church, alongside other children. He knew me well and appeared to be fond of me, until it transpired suddenly that it had all been a lie. I waited for what seemed an eternity. I remember being about to ask him what would be the repercussions of this revelation on my future in the church, but he suddenly said in a deep, somewhat breathy voice that, as a Jewish child, who had not been baptized into the church, I had committed a grave sin and was forbidden to taste the holy bread. He sounded horrified.

The priest managed eventually to gather his wits and after his dramatic declaration regarding my mortal sin, he admitted that it wasn't as bad as all that. He explained that I was still a child with pure intentions and since I had done all those things in order to save my life, I would not be punished for my misdeeds. He added that it was a pity that I was a Jew because he had felt that I was genuine in my actions. But since I was a Jew, the incident was closed and he for his part would be happy to help me if I needed help. The priest was a good-hearted and pleasant man and he played a major role in the lives of the children who attended his church. He even played football with us and we were all fond of him. I was surprised, therefore, that at the end of that conversation, he showed no sympathy towards me as a child who had done what he had done in order to save his life. He didn't ask about my parents, what had happened to them, nothing. He only expressed his regret that I had tasted the holy bread; after analyzing the situation he was relieved; and now, as far as he was concerned, his work was finished.

At that moment, I remembered the powerful urge that I had almost succumbed to when I had wanted to share the truth with him. It was clear to me now that since he was a good and merciful man he would not have betrayed me, but would almost certainly not have helped with anything, because he would have been too scared to move away from his closed and secure world. I believe he would have pretended not to hear and not to know. I wasn't annoyed with him. He was a good man who did only what was expected of him and we were all attached to him. He seemed sensitive when I returned to him one day after the previous confession and told him that I wished to be baptized a Christian. But, to my surprise, he wasn't very enthusiastic. Instead, he suggested I wait a while with so fateful a decision. He explained that I was, after all, a Jew "who had lost his way somewhat," and that we could discuss it further when things had settled down. He refrained from encouraging me to take this step and I remember this to his credit.

Things gradually settled into a pleasant routine. The neighborhood and our little house in the Brussels suburb started to fill with new people. René, Aunt Angele's son, was the first to arrive. Aunt Angele's husband, Uncle Francois, who returned from Britain, was next. I had never met him before and as soon as I saw him I felt a special affinity towards him. He was full of charm, was pleasant, good-hearted, patient and tolerant and he soon began treating me like his own son. He was softer than Aunt Angele and I enjoyed being around him. For the first time, we started to live like a family, each with his own agenda, but the evening meal we always ate together. René paid me a lot of attention and he helped me significantly to catch up with the schoolwork I had missed during the past two years because of my frequent absences from school. He also instructed me in subjects that I had practically no knowledge about and I made quite good progress. My teachers were also pleasant towards me. I reckon that they were aware of my "story," but they made no open reference to it. I was now a pupil like any other, doing my best to make up for lost time.

One day, two British soldiers appeared at our house. Aunt Angele received them cordially and invited them in. They sat and talked in the living room and in the course of the conversation, I learned that one of the two was Karl, the brother of Gretchen, my Uncle Paul's wife. I have already mentioned that Gretchen and Paul had managed to get out of Belgium, travelled across France and Spain, spent one year in Casablanca in Morocco and from there they were fortunate enough to get to the USA. I was very proud of the guests, the liberating war heroes, who had presented themselves in our home. I had a photograph taken with them, my lapel decorated with the flags of some of the Allied nations. Victory had taken on a new reality for me.

It soon transpired that Karl had not come to visit us by chance and that he was here on a mission on behalf of the "family." The word "family" echoed in my ears like some meaningless equation. Just a few months before, I had been all alone, fearful of every sound, surrounded by Aunt Angele's protective shadow — the only human being in the world who was on my side. Suddenly, I discovered that I had a family. I still didn't know what had happened to my parents or Aunt and Uncle. Karl wasn't familiar with all my family, but with restrained and typically British politeness, he explained that he knew that relatives of mine were scattered over countries and continents: in Israel, the United States and Europe, and that extensive correspondence was now being conducted among the relatives whose eyes were all on me. Until then, I had known nothing of all this. I later learned the details of their mission.

A meeting with Karl (left) and his friend, 1945. They were Allied soldiers who traced me to Brussels. On my lapel are flags of the allied countries.

Since he had arrived in Belgium with the British Armed Forces, my family had asked him to pay me a visit. Apparently, the only person who knew where I was located was Mr. Hourmont, as Aunt Angele was in contact with him. He never once came to visit me during the entire period I lived with Aunt Angele so as not to endanger us, nor did he say anything about it to my family for fear they would take steps that might endanger everyone. Throughout the war years none of my relatives, neither my grandmother nor my uncles, knew what had happened to me, whether I was alive or if I was in hiding. Only after Liberation did all this mechanism start to move and steps were taken, plans were drafted and decisions were made. All these took place around me, about me, and I didn't have a clue. After Liberation, Mr. Hourmont disclosed my location, presumably to my Uncle Avshalom in Haifa and to my grandmother, who was living in Jerusalem at the time. She had started to put things in motion, which is how Karl came to be visiting us with his friend, both in uniform. I suppose that Karl was quick to write to my grandmother with a detailed description of our meeting. Then there began a search for a home for me, under the firm leadership of my grandmother, Yocheved, my mother's mother.

A part of my return to normal life consisted of joining in the activities of the neighborhood children of my own age. Prompted by a powerful urge to be like other children and without even noticing it, I started to distance myself from the church and replaced it with the Scout movement, which became my main focus. Moreover, the battles fought against the neighborhood's Flemish children stopped — at least during the period following the war. At the end of the war, everyone wanted to go back to building a more suitable setup in which to conduct their "family life" in a way that was similar to what they had known in days gone by.

The war had upset everybody's lives, not only those of the Jews. Relatives were absent from their homes for extended periods, parents were busy with the day-to-day struggle for survival, the Allied bombs injured large numbers of the civilian population and caused considerable damage, tensions were high and the danger was real. In the atmosphere of uncertainty that prevailed during the war, children tended to be left to their own devices. They were able to run wild, to do anything that occurred to them and they were free of the beady eyes of their parents or other adults. When liberty came, life began to gradually return to normal and even people's free time showed signs of becoming established.

The Scout movement was a good and pleasantly convenient framework for many youngsters and I remember that most of my neighborhood friends joined. This was the first time in my life that I found myself in an organized youth movement, with counselors and commanders, most of whom were older than me and motivated by a pedagogic fervor and a thirst for activity. And indeed, I received my first lesson in citizenship in that group. Each evening I would return home to Aunt Angele; it was a real home to me, with a couple of adults — Aunt Angele and Uncle Francois — who behaved towards me as parents in every aspect. Previously, when I had been alone with Aunt Angele, I hadn't really had a sense of being "at home." Aunt Angele and I had done our best to turn the house into a warm and pleasant place, but with little success. Perhaps it was a result of the circumstances and the tensions they caused and the anxiety that required constant awareness; or perhaps it was due to Aunt Angele's restrained personality and the discipline she imposed on her feelings.

That summer she took me to a resort town called Middlekerke, on the North Sea coast, which was full of life after the prolonged stagnation of the war. It was the first time in my life I had been on vacation and to this day I remember it down to the smallest detail. We stayed in a small rented apartment and spent our days on the beach. I participated in children's contests: bicycle races, tug-of-war, running and many other games. The games took place along the length of the promenade and the local inhabitants and visitors celebrated into the night. There was an atmosphere of genuine release, and happiness flowed from the depths of people's hearts, with no one having to force it. It was actually the first vacation for everyone who came to Middlekerke that summer after a hiatus of more than five years. The unforgettable sights of those days, in a place that was devoted entirely to pleasure and *joie de vivre*, infused me with a great deal of energy and optimism.

On the last days of the vacation, Aunt Angele befriended a woman who had sat next to us a few times on the beach. The woman had a daughter of about the same age as me; I was ten at the time. I remember the girl's face to this day. She used to smile at me and I'd return her smile, even though I felt very embarrassed doing so. I spent a lot of time playing with other children during that vacation but for some reason, I didn't get the chance to play with her. I looked at her and when I felt her looking at me, too, I could feel a blush rising up my cheeks, which burned like fire. We barely exchanged a couple of words. Aunt Angele and the girl's mother tried to encourage us to play together, but we both remained planted where we were, exchanging stolen glances, blushing and lowering our eyes as if afraid of revealing some secret. The joy and freedom I felt during that vacation released hidden undercurrents in my heart and I seemed to have fallen in love with that girl. It probably happened because of the unique circumstances we were in; and since I was quite grown up for my age, I was mature enough to have such feelings. Perhaps it was also a yearning inside me for something deeper.

Playing tug-of-war during my first vacation in Middelkerke. I'm at the front. August 1945.

However, a problem always arose after we returned to our modest little vacation apartment. In the evenings, when we were alone with each other, my memories took me back to the dull reality of my life and filled me with sadness and despair. The sharp transition between my external joy and pleasure and my inner world was hard to bear and I sometimes felt a confused heaviness, which often awakened feelings of guilt that I was enjoying almost unfettered pleasure and setting free feelings and urges that I had managed hereto to repress. During the day, I was party to the joy and relaxation enjoyed by all the holidaymakers in Middlekerke, but in the evenings, alone with myself, I was gripped by a great sense of shame. This duality weighed heavily on me for many years before I eventually managed to free myself of it. But at that time, when I still believed that my parents would be returning to me after all, it was very difficult.

Several days after the end of the war we encountered the Belgian neighbor who had collaborated with the Germans and had "taken an interest" in me — as I have already mentioned — on several occasions. He appeared suddenly, riding a motorbike and passed quickly down our street. We kids noticed him and told the adults, who assumed he was practicing his motorbike skills so he could escape the minute he felt someone breathing down his neck. He was a loathsome man and the entire neighborhood hated him. We started to plot a scheme to get back at him and decided to scatter a lot of nails on the road. Traffic on our road was sparse in those days, so we could do this without fear of anyone else being hurt. After his second or third journey down our street, we heard him in the distance articulating a string of juicy curses.

To this day, I don't know if we caused him any damage, but we certainly enjoyed hearing that he was angry and, as children, that was all we were able to achieve. I don't know what ultimately happened to that vile man, but I do remember clearly that he disappeared and I believe his family did, too. At the same time, many of the neighbors were furious with some other people who lived among us and were suspected of having collaborated. I don't know how they were taken care of and I wasn't interested. I had an acute sense of the fury that emerged suddenly from the depths of these good people's hearts, who had suffered so much for so many years.

I continued to use my assumed family name during the first few months following the war, but over time, I returned to my original name. However, I don't remember if the change took place in Belgium or subsequently in France. The neighbors gradually learned that I was a Jew and that I had been in hiding at Aunt Angele's. Often a neighbor confided that he/she had actually suspected that that was the case. The story about me being the son of a distant relative of hers did indeed make sense, but I didn't really look Belgian and also I had been absent for long periods of time. It turned out that people had noticed and thought that things seemed a little strange; they had been neighbors of Aunt Angele and her husband for many years and the explanations for my sudden appearance seemed somewhat puzzling, to say the least. This was especially obvious among our closer neighbors.

As was typical in small neighborhoods, everyone knew everything there was to know about each other and I later learned that my friends in the group of Walloon kids had told their parents that I was often absent from their meetings and from school. I have no doubt that had we known this earlier, Aunt Angele would probably have tried to find a safer place for me to hide, which would have been to her benefit, too, since it transpired that she had been in greater danger than she realized. Quite simply, we were lucky since we were surrounded by good people. I remember, in particular, one close neighbor. She was an elderly woman who lived with her husband and a Pekinese dog. I never saw any children there and I never spoke to the couple, not even to say hello. They were discrete, quite reserved and I had the impression that they never paid any attention to me. They appeared very distinguished, always well dressed, leaving their home arm in arm. During the war, I had no fear of them. The war seemed not to affect them. They had a measure of self-satisfaction and there was a demonstrative calmness about them, but they never disturbed anyone and lived their lives at a distance from their surroundings. Oddly, it was the Pekinese that aroused my doubts. He was an angry, snappy creature and on the days I spent in my garden dugout I often worried that this little dog would start to make a fuss. But in the end, he did nothing, because he was locked inside the house most of the time.

This neighbor and Aunt Angele sometimes spoke to each other; although they had known each other for years, their relationship was very formal. And then, after the war ended, they chanced upon each other and the neighbor, who spoke first (as Aunt Angele told me later), said how glad she was that it had all ended well. Then she asked, "What is going to happen to the boy?" Aunt Angele questioned her carefully to find out what she meant and then the neighbor told her that she and her husband had been sure that the boy who appeared one fine day in the house next door had clearly "found shelter" in the home of their good-hearted neighbor, but they had decided not to discuss the matter. Only after the war did the neighbor decide to mention it to Aunt Angele and to tell her how much respect she had for her.

Some of the neighbors might have guessed at first that I was a Jew in hiding in the neighborhood under a false identity, but my lifestyle and church activity dispelled their suspicions to a certain extent and prompted them to leave me and Aunt Angele to our own devices. It also transpired after the war that my friends in the Walloon group had spoken about me, saying that I was very enthusiastic in our war games and that I was quite a quarrelsome kid. They had no way of understanding, of course, that I wasn't interested in the battles as such, but rather in the feeling of release and freedom that tended to dazzle me after the prolonged period in which I had been holed up at home with my parents and forbidden to make friends with other children. All this proves, in retrospect, that I had acted correctly and that my behavior had been interpreted more or less as I had wished. But still we were fortunate. We had also been fortunate because the adults had allowed their relations with each other to become quite lax. Each family tended to stay in its own home and deal with its own struggle for survival, leaving little room for gossip. There was no reason to take an interest in what was happening next door or across the street, except among such people that had turned it into an ideology, like the neighborhood collaborators. There had been several of those, but everyone had been wary of them. Since many of the collaborators acted clandestinely, other inhabitants preferred to be cautious and wary of everyone else.

No one fully trusted anyone else since it was impossible to tell who was a collaborator and who was not. This uncertainty caused considerable suffering to the adults, which is why they chose to keep to themselves. Many families broke up in some way or another. Some of the men joined the forces fighting against the Germans and were in London. Some were taken prisoner and others were killed. Also, some of the older boys disappeared after having been drafted into the Belgian Army. In many families, the woman of the house assumed full responsibility and it was around her that everything rotated. The mother's main objective was the survival of her family — to find food and to make some kind of a living in order to enable the others to keep afloat. This was probably the reason why our neighbors didn't try too hard to solve the mystery of my sudden appearance at Aunt Angele's.

It became apparent with time that certain neighbors had actually noticed me. They had heard things about me from their children, but were not interested in learning more due to fear for their safety. People were afraid to know too much, were fearful of discovering new things. They were all aware of their duty to report to the authorities on any deviation they came across, i.e., to inform on someone. Everyone knew very well, not least from the experience of others, that any contact with the authorities led to being registered with them, and all that this entailed. People who had been reported had to undergo harsh interrogations and were often instructed to report back to the authorities. From the moment they were registered they were "catalogued" and required to prove to the authorities that their motives were honorable and that all they had wanted was to fulfill their civil duty "to the best of their ability."

Since the inhabitants were cautious with regard to the authorities, the authorities in turn were increasingly suspicious vis-à-vis the civilian population. It was a very complex system and one to be expected when part of the population collaborates "discreetly" with the occupying forces, which was the case with the Belgian police. The paralyzing fear that gripped the Belgian people seems to have played a huge part in my secret not being revealed. However, the rules of the game changed completely once the war was over. Since families had more or less rehabilitated their lives, they were free to begin to slowly peel away the thick layers of suspicion that had covered them and to take a genuine interest in what was happening around them. People opened their hearts and talked about what they had been through and they gradually reformed neighborly relations, which then developed into even deeper and more open friendships.

In the latter half of 1945, some feverish activity started to take place concerning what was going to happen to me, and quite a few people were involved in this. The timing for this did not really suit me, since, at long last, I had started to feel comfortable around Aunt Angele and her husband, Francois, who cared for and was devoted to me. Their twenty-year-old son René had brought home his girlfriend, Suzette, a charming young woman, beautiful and educated and full of *joie de vivre*. René, who tried to help me with my homework, was young, energetic, generous and spirited, but he was also impatient. I would often irritate him when I was unable to grasp the meaning of things he was trying to explain to me. At such times, Suzette would take over from him. She would treat me like a slightly difficult pupil, in need of consideration and patience. Most of the time, her soft, maternal and friendly approach bore fruit with the achievement of better results. Naturally, this had a positive effect on my feelings and on my successful integration into the lives of the family and the neighborhood. However, notwithstanding the pleasant routine that my life followed during this period, I never ceased my efforts to locate my parents and my Uncle Salo and Aunt Hanna'le. Aunt Angele and her family did their best to help me and stood firmly and unconditionally by me. But it all extracted from me so much emotional energy. My life seemed to move along on two levels — the permanent and the temporary — between which I found a middle-of-the-road approach, and thus, my future did not appear so frightening.

Subsequently, I found out about the activity surrounding my fate. The decision on my future had been entrusted solely to my grandmother in Israel. Grandmother Yocheved, a controlling and opinionated woman, handled affairs in a high-handed manner. Her two sons in the US and the one in Israel were as obedient as ever and what she said was law. Her preference was for me to move to the

US to live with my uncles there. She believed that life in New York would be the best option for me. Of course, both my uncles agreed to take me, but there was a condition: I would have to work in order to finance my schooling, since they were themselves newly-arrived immigrants living on low incomes and unable to add another child to their families. This stipulation, however, was not acceptable to my grandmother.

As a woman who had continued to behave like a Viennese matriarch throughout her time in Israel, through periods of harsh austerity, it didn't occur to her that her grandson would have to work to pay for his education. My uncle in Israel, Avshalom, and his wife, Pnina, also wanted to have a say in the fateful decision and asked to adopt me, despite their difficult financial situation at that time. My uncle wanted me to be raised in Israel, as their own son in every way, alongside their own sons, Zvi and Yigal. But my grandmother rejected this solution out of hand. She had a negative attitude to Israel and she firmly refused to accept this proposal. However, as time passed, Uncle Avshalom started to oversee the formal process of bringing me to Israel.

At some stage in the process another person, who until then had been unfamiliar to me, became involved. My Aunt Hilda from France firmly and unreservedly informed my grandmother that she wished to give me a home. I only learned the details of this later. As soon as she and her husband learned that I had survived, they wanted to take me into their home. They promised my grandmother that they would raise me alongside their only daughter, with no distinction, in every way as their own son. In the end, this proposal was the one that was acceptable to my grandmother and the decision was made. In her heart, my grandmother wanted her grandson to receive a European education and this was now achievable. Aunt Angele informed me of the decision and thus my fate was sealed once again.

The decision fell upon me suddenly and, as I have said, the timing was bad. An emotional storm raged deep inside me. Although I was only ten years old, I felt grown up and master of my destiny in terms of having experience in making big decisions on my own. I consulted with Aunt Angele, and her advice helped me to weigh my options, but not to decide on them. In fact, when I encountered problems, I would try to think how my father would have dealt with them, how he would have acted and what he would have decided. As far as I was concerned, at that time he was and remained to be my main source of authority. And here, when I was already ten years old, aware of my ability to survive and carefully analyzing every move in my life, I found myself all of a sudden totally lacking any status, devoid of all authority and denied all rights.

The whole world was considering what was best for me; strangers were determining my future. No one asked me what I thought and no one consulted me. This angered me considerably and gave me a negative attitude vis-à-vis any decision taken on my behalf, a kind of all-inclusive objection to everything and everyone. I suffered badly from everything that was happening around me. Aunt Angele, a gentle woman who had become very attached to me, behaved with utmost consideration, but in the end she had little say in the matter. All the consultations were conducted among my relatives under the authoritarian baton of my grandmother. Aunt Angele would have wanted me to remain with her, I felt sure of that.

To be honest, I was very excited when a connection — initially only through correspondence — was made between my family and me after the war. I suddenly felt enveloped by a kind of warmth. No longer was I alone in the world. Here, I have relatives who knew my parents. This feeling was very helpful in coping with the "existential loneliness" that I had been carrying within me for the last two years, since the disappearance of my family. I felt a kind of euphoria when it became clear that I now had a connection with my roots. I went back to being me, reassumed my real name and acknowledged that I was an Austrian-born Jew, with a grandmother, uncles, aunts and cousins. It all took me back to a past that appeared so far away and hazy, to the extent that I couldn't tell what was real and what was imagined.

Nevertheless, this renewed connection with my family that thrilled me so much, also awakened in me serious misgivings and considerable confusion. After two years, during which I was someone else, I was forced to return to the real me and to erase that chapter in my life that suddenly seemed to belong to somebody else. Those had been years of absolute change; not only of my name, religion and family history, but also a fundamental change of identity, the adoption of a world that had not been mine, that was foreign to me, a world I had been obliged to embed within me in order to survive. Within this total transformation, I made sure to preserve a tiny opening into the real past. I had known all along who I was, and in my heart I had established an altar to my parents and to my aunt and uncle, who had once been my entire world; but I also adopted my present with open arms. The false identity that had allowed me to survive was dear to me. At that time, I had no objection to remaining a Christian Belgian boy living with Aunt Angele.

Following a lengthy correspondence, it was determined that I would move to my aunt's home in France. This was my grandmother's ruling and no one dared appeal her decision. At the same time, it was decided to embark on a process that would allow me to join my new family already in April 1946, after my eleventh birthday. My last months in Belgium were hard on me. I wanted time to stop; I didn't want to think that these were my final months in a world that had become my own. I remember the growing number of days when I refused to go to school, preferring to stay alone in my room in order to "spend a little time with my parents." I felt suddenly that I was deserting them, too. They, too, belonged to this place; they had brought me there. They had known Aunt Angele. In this room, I had spent countless hours with their memory. It was my only connection with my past and now this, too, was about to be taken away from me. The search for my parents and my uncle and aunt had failed dismally and I started to understand that they were never going to return. These were my feelings when Aunt Angele and her husband Francois informed me that a decision had been made and I was to travel to France to the home of some aunt I had never met.

I had been naïve enough to believe that I was capable of passing any test I was confronted with. I was sure that I had the strength to cope with any hardship and danger. I had full confidence in my emotional resilience and ability to deal with any circumstances that required improvisation, composure and self-discipline. After all, I had experienced numerous incidents in which I was required to don the necessary armor to defend myself. I knew I had to beware of people and had developed sensors that enabled me to size them up when necessary. I was careful of people, but not afraid of them. Now, suddenly, I felt that all the defense systems I had built for myself collapsed at once. The armor turned to mush. The tough boy I had been, the boy who was used to manipulating those around him, became a softie, an orphan, devoid of self, dependent on others. From a creature who believed that he had control over his fate I became a boy who caves in without putting up a fight to the decisions of a grandmother he had never even met.

The situation seemed illogical, but I felt like a cripple, unable to respond. Grandmother spoke, decided and ruled and I, an obedient and submissive boy, accepted her sentence. I was ashamed of myself. How could she and my uncles decide what was good for me; they didn't even know me. Everything inside me protested. So why didn't I react, rebel, resist? I seem to have succumbed to a feeling of helplessness, the weakness of a child against the adult world. I was also alone and withdrawn and, to a certain extent, I had become caught up in a passive mindset. I was tired of the constant weight of responsibility and placed my fate in the hands of others, of adults.

I sometimes imagined that I would find refuge in the Christian religion. I believed then that prayer could influence and change things to my benefit. However, I soon understood that there was nothing certain in this. Aunt Angele sensed my suffering and tried hard to explain my situation to me. She explained that nothing was more natural than for a person to return and rejoin his source, even if for some time his fate had removed him from it. She did her absolute best to instill in me some hope and faith. And yet, because I knew her so well, I felt that she was doing it unenthusiastically, almost painfully. Aunt Angele was the only person whose authority I was prepared to accept, because she had been at my side for more than two years and had risked her life for me. She knew perfectly what was happening inside me. She had cracked my code. Therefore, since Aunt Angele advised me to act according to my grandmother's ruling, I surrendered. Her argument that both she and I were obliged to behave in accordance with my family's instructions persuaded me. Thus, another chapter in my life came to an end.

Towards the end of the war, a lively correspondence took place between Belgium and Israel with regard to my future. Here is a brief selection:

### Letter from Mr. Hourmont to Uncle Avshalom

*Brussels, March 15, 1945*

*I am happy to be able at long last to make contact with the people closest to little Henri, in the event that his parents never return. Henri's mother told me a lot about your mother. I know that my news will pain her, but it will be a relief for her to know that the boy has survived. I would ask you to inform her that her daughter and son-in-law thought about her a lot even during the most difficult periods.*

*Your sister and her family lived in my house from the beginning of 1941 and her brother and his wife lived not far from here. They sometimes had to leave their apartment and take refuge in other apartments. In the summer of 1942, your brother and his wife were asked by the Germans to report to Malines and, against my advice, they responded to this summons and went there on their own counsel. At about the same time, I was obliged to take the boy to the hospital, together with his mother, after he broke his arm in the course of a game. Since the Germans followed patients who had been hospitalized, I registered him as my own son. He never again saw his uncle and aunt, who disappeared completely. At about that time the Germans intensified their unannounced visits, which forced your family to be absent for lengthy periods. About a year after your brother and his wife were summoned to Malines, your sister and her husband were captured. The authorities also searched for the boy, but fortunately, your sister had managed to find him a hiding place several months beforehand. I have kept some objects belonging to them and, of course, I hope they return home and that I can give everything back to them.*

*In everything concerning the boy, I suggest you don't rush into writing to me. The war is about to end and it would be a pity to take hasty steps. There is still room for caution. I am full of hope that Henri's parents and uncle and aunt will return and they can all be together again. Naturally, I shall inform you of any positive development in this tragic issue.*

*Yours truly,*
*Octave Hourmont*

**Letter from Uncle Avshalom to Aunt Angele**

*Haifa, May 18, 1945*

*Just a few days ago I received a letter from my brothers in America with the news that my nephew Henri is staying with you. We would like to thank you for saving his life. I am at a loss for words to express our gratitude for your magnanimity during this so difficult period. We shall never forget your generosity. We have been enormously fortunate in having you to care for the boy and we are very sorry that we have only words with which to reciprocate. We have only recently been made aware by Mr. Hourmont of the tragedy that has befallen our family, but he did not mention where Henri is located. My brothers have now informed me where he is.*

*The entire family is currently involved in this [matter]. My brothers in America are making great effort in order to bring him to them. I, too, am trying to prepare all the documents [necessary] for bringing him to Israel. Whichever one of us succeeds will take care of him. In January of this year, I registered the boy here in [British Mandate] Palestine at the immigration offices. Now that I have been informed that his name has been changed, I have registered him under his new name, DIEUDONNÉ. I hope that Mr. Hourmont will be in contact with the Zionist Federation and they will contact Henri. Recently a special delegation left here in order to deal with the immigration of [Jewish] children from France and Belgium to [British Mandate] Palestine and I am full of hope that our little Henri will be among them. I would greatly appreciate a detailed account of his condition. How is he? Does he attend school? Does he remember his parents? My brother wrote me that he has sent you several food parcels. Unfortunately, we are unable to send anything, since it is forbidden to send parcels from [British Mandate] Palestine. Of course, the moment the situation changes, we, too, will send you [parcels]. Please write to me as much as you can about the boy and we shall keep you in the picture. We here are all hoping to see him soon.*

*Please accept our warmest greetings,*
*Avshalom*

## Letter from Uncle Avshalom to me

*A few words to you. We have recently been informed that you have remained alone in Belgium. I have written a few letters to Hourmont, but I think he has not given them to you [...]. We are doing our best to bring you here and we hope that it won't be long until we can see each other. Kisses from me, from Aunt Pnina and your two cousins, Zvika and Yigal.*

*Waiting for you,*
*Your Uncle Adolf (Avshalom)*

## Letter from me to my grandmother

*Brussels, June 12, 1945*

*Dear Grandmother,*
*It is very kind of you to invite me to live with you; but I would prefer to stay here with Aunt Angele. If I do come to you, it will be too far for Mother and Father to come to take me. And if I see them again, we shall all come to visit you. I am happy here with*

*Aunt Angele. I do a lot of sport, play tennis and football and I
have started attending the Scouts. I am also studying music and
have been singing for several years already. I hope you are all
feeling well and that we can meet soon.*

*Your grandson*
*Henri*

## Letter from Mr. Hourmont to Uncle Avshalom

*Brussels, July 6, 1945*

*You seem not to understand why Henri is living with the lady
he refers to as Aunt Angele. So, here is the explanation for this
matter. His parents lived on the second story of my house together
with their son. When the Germans began their persecution of the
Jews, the family went into hiding in various houses, each time
for a certain period, until the worst would be over. I advised
them to separate from the boy and seek a safer place for him
and, indeed, this is what happened, even if a little late. After
Henri was already in hiding, I had four visits from the Germans,
one after the other. On one of these visits, I was obliged to sign
– under threat of death – that I knew nothing about the location
of the parents and the boy. Your sister had visited me a few days
earlier and gave me several addresses, including yours, and
asked me to inform you if anything happened to them. She also
asked me to protect the child, albeit from a distance, but that I
take care of him later and this I am doing now.*

*At the moment, Henri is on vacation by the sea, behaving
well and is content. Unfortunately, he has a problem with his
arm. As I have already written to you, he broke his arm when
he was still living with his parents, which makes me think that
his bones are too soft. Through the offices of various mediators,
I have made contact with your brothers in America and, as a
result, a British soldier who introduced himself as your brother-
in-law visited me.*

*I am very happy that Henri's grandmother is with you and feeling well. On the matter of her daughter and son who are still missing, she must continue to hope. There is a rumor that many Jews are still imprisoned in Russia. Thus, there is no meaning to the fact that no news has been received so far. Believe me, there is no reason to start moving the boy at this time. Here in Belgium he feels at home. We would have been happy had we been able to do for other children all that we did for Henri. The fact is that many [Jewish] children have been saved by Christian institutes such as convents and churches. We did everything we could under the harsh circumstances.*

*Since you have already offered, we would be very happy to receive food parcels for the boy. I hope the situation here will improve very soon. I am including a photograph of Henri.*

*Yours truly,*
*Octave Hourmont*

# CHAPTER THREE

## *HILDA AND MILEK*

In April 1946, I travelled to France with Aunt Angele. The train stopped in Paris and we had some time in which to wander through the streets before boarding the train that would take us to our final destination. Aunt Angele was dressed in her very best clothes, while I was travelling in my Scout uniform. I was proud to belong to the Scout troop in my Brussels neighborhood. It would never have occurred to me to turn up at my relatives' home looking like a refugee being shunted from place to place, but as a free boy, a member of a well-known, international youth movement. Hence, I decided to wear my uniform. And another thing: Although I had objected to being passed on to a new family I was unfamiliar with, which, in the end, I accepted as the ruling, in my eyes, that uniform was an expression of my absolute independence. Also, there is no denying the message that I internalized during the war — a uniform is tantamount to power and imparts a certain glory to its wearer. So, I may well have found it important to make my first appearance dressed in my splendid uniform, rather than as a downtrodden orphan. Aunt Angele made no objection to this little idiosyncrasy, and so it was. My new family welcomed me most warmly and Aunt Angele stayed on for two or three days before returning to Brussels.

The separation from her was extremely difficult. She had been everything to me. I knew that she was taking with her some of my secrets and most intimate feelings, although we had never actually had a real conversation about them. She had known my parents. We had been through some harsh experiences together; together we had withstood tests that tightened the connection between us. And then, when I was beginning to feel that she was my real family and that she was the most appropriate soul to fill some of the void left by my parents, we were separated forever. She wept when we said our goodbyes, deep, silent tears that expressed a genuine pain. Years later, while mulling this over, I felt that I had been a tragic hero. Giant forces had shaken my life and determined my fate. I understood that there was no point in fighting them because the results had been predestined; the verdict had already been passed. Aunt Angele and I were pawns in a power game to determine my fate — the main players in this case being my biological family, especially my grandmother. Deep inside I was in turmoil over my decision to acquiesce to my grandmother's dictates, a woman I didn't even know. In fact, I didn't know a single person from all those who were huddled beneath that umbrella that was defined as "family."

During my first few days with my new family I felt an utter lack of belonging to the world around me. My brain was rife with thoughts and feelings of guilt: I had been defeated by the grownups. I was troubled unrelentingly by the question: Should I, after all, have shown more resistance? Things were not clear enough to me and I remember being miserable. I didn't connect with my new surroundings. It was very difficult for me to adjust to a different family environment, into which I was required to adapt to an already organized and predictable daily routine, where meals were eaten at set times and the manners and etiquette were alien to me. There had been no real framework in my parents' home, by nature and because of the war. Survival had been the name of the game and it took place within a closed and intimate space. Every day was an entirely new world — the struggle, the hardship and the semi-secret setup in which we existed. All these had provided me with much warmth and had tightened the physical and emotional connection between us. We lived in constant anxiety and our concern for each other was existential.

Later, at Aunt Angele's, I had turned into a different kind of child. I had adopted a mode of behavior and lifestyle that were compatible with my new identity — from a Jew-in-hiding I became a Christian kid, paving a different path and forging a place for myself in a new society and a new environment. All these, along with the daily struggle against events, each one of which could have been critical, brought about changes in my personality. I turned into a very independent, quite outgoing boy, at least outwardly. For over two years I spent more time in the streets than in the house. But, I did have my boundaries. Discipline was the fruit of my own decision — the discipline of an adult who is aware of the special boundaries his life is subject to. And thus, my life continued like this throughout the war. Once the war was over, I was a regular kid adjusting to his new circumstances with a close connection to his "family" and to the neighborhood in which his life had been saved. In those days, this connection, which was free of anxiety and based on choice, love and on a shared past, was the only stable thing in my life. And at exactly that time, it was decided that I was to set off once again on a lengthy journey, to be someone else once again, to become accustomed to people I had never met before and to accept their laws, their behavior and their authority. The hardest thing of all was the need to relinquish the independence I had known in Belgium, which is why I suffered so much during the first part of my stay in France.

From the moment I had been severed from my nuclear family, the yearning for connection had held my constant attention. At first, I felt alienation towards Aunt Angele and I tried my hardest to hold onto the umbilical cord that tied me to my family. But, as time passed and it became apparent that my parents were not going to return — at least for the duration of the war — I gradually formed a connection with Aunt Angele that grew ever closer. The logic that led to this step was rooted in the knowledge that Aunt Angele had known my parents. This is what enabled the connection between her and me and the dangers we were constantly in only reinforced it. The idea of having other family somewhere did not trouble me at all at that time. My day-to-day life wrung my strength and my thoughts dry, so that I had no time left for such thoughts. In any case, I had no recollection of my grandmother or uncles. But the thoughts of my circumstances as a child devoid of roots began to trouble me towards the end of the war, when I suddenly felt a loss of direction.

My wartime identity suited me better than my real one, although deep inside I knew that eventually I would have to deal with this issue as well. The knowledge that I had been left all alone troubled my thoughts more than my feelings. I was surrounded by children with parents, brothers, sisters and other family members, which soon led me to understand that, to a certain degree, I was different. So, I started to lean on my new family — Aunt Angele and Uncle Francois — and really tried to be consumed by it. After the war, the news that a connection had been made with my biological family made me happy at first. The thought of my maternal grandmother being alive and taking an interest in me actually warmed my heart and excited me. But she and her son in Israel were strangers to me; and I was unable to muster any interest in my aunt in France and actually developed a genuine hostile attitude towards her and her family.

Our neighborhood in Brussels consisted of small houses surrounded by greenery. The houses were not fancy, but full of color. The inhabitants were low- to middle-class and mostly very pleasant, warm-hearted, simple people. I knew every road, every cul-de-sac and almost every yard. The neighborhood was friendly and I felt like I belonged there. The French city I later arrived in, on the other hand, appeared gloomy, gray and almost hostile. The buildings were tall, neglected on the outside and blackened by soot from the coal mines that surrounded them. A day after our arrival, Aunt Angele and I went on a tour of the city center. We were both horrified, but Aunt Angele wasn't about to admit it; naturally enough, she didn't want to cause me any more pain. Her impression of the place was obviously the same as mine: It all looked so old, ancient even.

We felt like strangers; but on that trip we were together and I felt less of the loneliness one feels in an unfamiliar environment. In our neighborhood in Brussels, there were always only a few people on the streets, whereas here, there was a lively movement of pedestrians rushing on their way to somewhere, no one looked anyone else in the eye and everyone seemed gloomy and ensconced in his own little shell: They appeared as stern, closed people. Even when some of them stood chatting on a street corner, they appeared formal and chilly with each other. Aunt Angele and I didn't exchange so much as a word. We were each engrossed in his or her personal contemplations regarding the new situation, but said nothing. In the past, too, we had not shared our impressions of things connected to our frame of mind. There had always been a silent understanding between us, and at that moment, we were in total agreement and both felt a kind of oppression, the memory of which remains carved within me to this very day.

The family unit of which I was now a part consisted of three people — father, mother and only daughter, Annette. The mother, whom I called Aunt Hilda, was actually my first cousin. She was my father's oldest sister's daughter and over 20 years my senior. I called her "aunt" because of the large age difference between us.

Aunt Hilda, Poland 1935.

She had been very close to my father when she was a girl, and was therefore motivated to suggest to my grandmother that she should adopt me into her family. Aunt Hilda was born in Galicia shortly before the outbreak of World War One. At that time, Galicia was part of the Austro-Hungarian Empire. After graduating from the local high school, she went on to study German language and literature at the university in Stanislavov, not far from Lvov.[13] Hilda was her parents' only daughter and had grown up pampered and full of charm, surrounded by three brothers in a well-to-do family. On a summer vacation in Zakopane — a well-known holiday resort in Poland — she met and fell in love with a young Jewish veterinarian called Milek, who was also vacationing there.

Milek was born at the beginning of the twentieth century in Lvov, the large and impressive capital of Galicia. His family was well off. Both his elementary and high school education were conducted in German, since the country was under Austrian control at the time. After graduating from high school, Milek wanted to study medicine, but this was denied him because of the restrictions imposed at that time on Jews. In Poland, a quota had been determined for the number of Jews eligible to study medicine (*numerus clausus* in Latin or "closed number") and there was no longer any place for him. Since Milek had no interest in moving to another country, he decided to study veterinary medicine instead. He completed his studies in Lvov and graduated with a prestigious degree in Veterinary Surgery.

With his small retroussé nose, medium build and straight back, Milek didn't look Jewish. He had a strong and determined personality and the manners of a gentleman. He was also a very proud and courageous man and, as a result, he was drawn on several occasions to participate in a duel, a form of combat prevalent in the German and Austrian universities of his time. The reason for these conflicts was usually due to an insult hurled at one of the participants or an

13   Until the end of World War I, Eastern Galicia had been part of the Austro-Hungarian Empire. It was returned to independent Poland in the period between the two worlds wars. From 1939 to 1941, it fell under the control of the Soviet Union. Since the end of World War II, it has been part of Ukraine.

affront to his honor, but more often than not, the cause was romantic. Milek was a skilled swordsman and always came out of these contests unscathed. Uncle Milek — as I called him — had another interesting trait: He was ambidextrous; his left hand was as nimble and as skilled as his right. This was deemed a great advantage and years later it would be very useful when he performed surgery on animals. He really was considered an exceptionally successful surgeon.

On completing his studies, Milek enlisted in the Polish Army and served in the cavalry. He learned to ride horses and, at the same time, he learned how to fight in battle. One of his achievements from this period in his life, about which he often boasted, was the ability to roll a cigarette from a miniscule piece of paper, with a couple of pieces of crumbled tobacco leaf on top, while riding a horse. He used to lay the tobacco on the piece of paper and roll it with one hand, using his thumb and several other fingers, his other hand holding the horse's reins. Following a few months of training, Milek was summoned to take exams for officer training. He was surprised, since Jews were not usually admitted to the officer ranks. And indeed, he soon discovered that his enrollment in the officer training course had been based on a mistake.

Milek had the same surname, which didn't have a necessarily Jewish ring to it, as another soldier in his unit. Since Milek looked like a gentile and the other soldier who, although a Christian, looked like a Jew, the military authorities assumed that Milek was the chosen candidate and promptly called him up for the exams. Milek decided not to reveal the mistake to anyone and, after taking and passing all the exams, he was accepted for officer training in the Polish Army. Once they discovered the "tragic" mistake, the military authorities tried to undo the damage, but the determined and stubborn Milek refused to budge and demanded to remain on the course. For many months, he suffered from various forms of harassment but he didn't give in and he completed the course, graduating as an officer. All the unpleasant episodes that Milek experienced as a boy and as a young man led him to the conclusion that he had no future in Poland and he decided to immigrate to France. This saddened his parents and siblings, who tried to dissuade him from taking this step, but Milek was determined to act on his decision and moved to France. He was the only member of his extensive family to survive the Holocaust.

In the first chapter of his life in France, Milek settled in late 1920s Paris. Although he had a degree in Veterinary Surgery, he was required to retake the final year of the course in Paris. He registered at the National Veterinary School of Maisons-Alfort — the best-known institution of its kind in France — and invested much time and effort in learning French. It wasn't easy for him, but he managed to pass all his exams and a year later, Milek had gained his diploma, a license to work in France and a reasonable command of the French language. He began working in a suburban town and a relatively short time afterwards, he came across an official call for young vets to apply for an interesting position in one of the French colonies. Milek made inquiries and discovered that the position was an attractive one in the West African country of Senegal. On the spot, he decided to apply for the job, won the appointment and sailed to Senegal. It was around 1931 and within a short while he was appointed Chief Veterinary Surgeon in Senegal as well as another country, which was known then as French Sudan and is now called Mali.

In 1933, Milek made a "home visit" to Poland and stayed in the resort town of Zakopane, where wealthy Jews habitually spent their vacations. It was there that he met and fell in love with Hilda, who also liked to spend her vacations there. After a brief engagement, the two married and Hilda accompanied him to Africa, which was quite a daring thing to do in those days. Hilda was young and pampered, but it seemed that her love for the young man knew no bounds and overcame all obstacles. It had been love at first sight for the young couple, as Hilda testified dozens of times (Milek was more reserved and reticent on matters of the heart). The young couple set up home in Tambacounda, a small township near the border between Senegal and Mali. This location allowed Milek relatively easy access to both countries for which he was responsible for veterinary services.

Life in Africa was not easy in the least. My aunt and uncle managed to contract diseases such as malaria and had to contend with countless insects and animals as well as various kinds of reptiles, of which there were plenty in the vicinity of their home. On various occasions they were victims of robbery, theft and abuse. Despite the harsh living conditions in Africa that were hard on Hilda, Milek was a happy man, with status and employment in an interesting position. For the first time, he was being treated as a human being and a veterinarian, and not only as a Jew. His French was fluent and he felt in every way a Frenchman. The vast open spaces of Africa gave him a sense of freedom and he had no intention of returning to the densely populated, oppressive and antisemitic Europe. He would speed along in his large car over unfamiliar dirty and dusty roads; and it was he who determined the routes and dictated the rules. Everywhere and at all times he was accompanied by a primeval feeling that brought with it a sense of spiritual uplift. In the past, he had been obliged to wage a constant struggle against his environment, to weigh each and every step he took, to carefully choose every word. Africa provided him with a world that was open and wild that suited his feisty and independent personality and he declared on several occasions that had it been possible, he would have continued to live in Africa for the rest of his life.

Years later, when I was already a university student, I decided to travel to Africa to follow the route of my Uncle Milek's life in the black continent some 30 years earlier. This trip was for me something of a roots journey. I believed it would bring me even closer to him and I tried to understand what had motivated him to build his future in this part of the world that was so far away from his own origins. Towards the end of 1934, a now-pregnant Hilda decided that she would not give birth to their first child in an African jungle, but in Poland, in the bosom of her loving and pampering family. Thus, she went back to Poland and Annette, their daughter, was born in January 1935 in Polish Galicia. From then on, the birth of their daughter dictated the family's future. Hilda informed Milek unequivocally that life in Africa with a small baby was out of the question. She was prepared to remain in Poland or, alternatively, if Milek so wished, to settle in France. Hence, Hilda and the baby girl immigrated to France. Hilda's entire family (which was also my father's family) perished in the Holocaust.

For Milek, the departure from Africa was painful and, for the rest of his life, he never ceased yearning for it. The young family decided to establish their home in a suburban town in France, several

Uncle Milek in Africa, 1935.

hundred kilometers from Paris. As happens with many immigrants, their choice of location was not random. They chose to live near a childhood friend of Milek's from Lvov, an engineer, who had found work in the town some years earlier and recommended the place.

At first, Milek worked in the clinic of a local well-established veterinarian until, not long after, he decided to open a clinic of his own. He treated small domestic animals there and made house calls to the farms that surrounded the town. Since he had a special affinity for horses and was experienced in treating them, he became recognized in the region as the number one expert on horse diseases.

In 1939, with the outbreak of World War II, Milek was drafted into the French Army as Veterinary Corps Officer, but was released several months later. On returning home, Milek, with his family, went into hiding in a town not far from their hometown. However, he was arrested towards the end of the war and taken to Drancy, a transit camp near Paris, where Jews were brought before being transported to the extermination camps. However, good fortune smiled on him and, just a few days before the Germans had time to deport him, the war ended.

This was the family I went to live with in April 1946, when I was 11 years old. Their daughter, Annette, was my age and already attending high school, since the average age of entry was 11. She was a slightly plump, very pretty girl, with black hair and black eyes, with a mischievous trait but still a good girl and a good student, who also played the piano. I resented her from the first time I set eyes on her — for the way she looked, her success in school, her musical talents and her captivating personality. To me, she was a symbol of everything a child can aspire to, with all the qualities I did not possess. I was very jealous of who she was and what she represented. Aside from all that, there was the feeling of alienation. Annette felt at home, whereas I really didn't. I felt bad, inferior, that I didn't belong and I was angry. As time went by, my longing for Aunt Angele grew stronger and during those moments when I was on my own and unoccupied, I often thought of running away and returning to Brussels.

Before leaving Brussels I had a very serious conversation with the priest at my church. I have already mentioned that I had asked him to baptize me. The priest listened carefully to my request, but took his time responding to it. He explained that I was Jewish, as were my parents and all the rest of my family and that it was not a good idea to take such a fateful and significant step without first taking some time out to think the matter through and to decide whether this was the right thing for me to do. He advised me to postpone the decision, to carefully weigh up all the repercussions, perhaps to discuss it with some of my family members and only then to act. I was not particularly persuaded by what he said, and since he seemed in no hurry to give in to my pressure, I asked him for a letter of referral to a priest in the town to which I was about to be moving. He agreed to draft such a letter and handed it to me a few days before I left for France.

He wrote in the letter that I was a Jewish boy who had masqueraded as a Catholic during the war in order to escape German persecution and that I intended to convert to Christianity. He added that I was an orphan and would be joining my Jewish family in France. The letter also included a detail that I considered of great importance and was indeed accurate — that I wished wholeheartedly to become a missionary in Africa and to devote my life to deprived people. This really was my life's desire. It would seem that the priest in Brussels was impressed by the strength of my wishes and was convinced of the sincerity of my intentions. It went without saying that the conversation and the letter were to remain a secret; no one was to know about them except the two of us.

The day after Aunt Angele's departure from France, while the four of us were having dinner, I pulled out the letter from my pocket and showed it to Uncle Milek. He read it with interest, passed it over to his wife and asked her to read it. Aunt Hilda read the letter and, from the depths of her heart, there emerged the words, "*Oh, mon dieu.*" (Oh, my God.) I saw my uncle give her a look that was at once horrified and beseeching. He turned, scrutinized me and said in a quiet, assuring voice, "It is quite alright." He added that we could show the letter to the priest when the time came, but there was no need to rush and it would be best to wait until I had acclimatized to my new home and environment.

Of course, by the time I understood the extent of the commotion I had caused, I was quite satisfied. But at that time, it was what I aspired to, because I didn't like those people who were suddenly made responsible for my entire future. "I want to see a priest, because at this moment it's the most important thing in my life. I miss the church. I wish to be a part of it and to tie my destiny to it," I claimed with determination. It was as if a bomb had dropped in the elegant dining room. Aunt Hilda stood up from the table for a moment as if intending to fetch the next course. As for Milek, he made no move whatsoever, but looked helpless. Annette glanced over at me and appeared amused by what had just happened at the table. Hilda returned with a plate of cooked vegetables, which she placed in the middle of the table and started serving some to everyone. Then, Milek said in a deep, slightly hoarse voice, "I can understand your fervor, my dear Henri. We shall respect your wishes, as I have told you, but let's take it step by step," and added in his gruff voice, "I promise you this." He went on to explain his reasoning, saying, "There are, after all, other things that need dealing with, maybe even more urgent things. We'll sit down and discuss them, we'll examine them together and, together, we'll try to solve all the issues." And then he said with a smile, "We've heard that you are a talented boy and I am sure that everything will go quickly. I promise you again that nothing will be done without consulting you. You'll be included in every decision we make and we will implement it only if it is acceptable to you."

My uncle's appeasing voice was reassuring and I let the matter rest for the time being, but I couldn't avoid noticing how hard it was for my aunt to hide her emotions. Over time, I learned to understand the reason for Aunt Hilda's upset when she first heard of my intention to convert to Christianity. Aunt Hilda had loved my father more than her other siblings and her memory of him as an observant Jew and the son of a rabbi was extremely dear to her. So, the idea of his son becoming a Christian was no less than sacrilege that shook her to her foundations. I have no doubt that the memory of her own family perishing in the Holocaust affected her as profoundly. Still, I didn't drop the subject and found an original way of showing my conviction. From that day on, at the beginning of every meal, I would cross myself provocatively at the table. I would bring my hand down from my forehead to my chest and continue by taking it to my left shoulder and from there to the right shoulder, in a single slow and concerted action.

I think I must have been trying to show them that I was not going to surrender easily to the rules of their home, combined with a yearning to preserve something of my past in Brussels. I don't remember ever having crossed myself at Aunt Angele's. I daresay she would have pointed out that this was not something my parents would have wanted and she would probably not have taken kindly to my becoming a Christian. So long as there was a war going on, the circumstances dictated my behavior, but as soon as it was over, she would certainly have demanded that I return to my original religion. As much as she understood that I was required to attend church during the war, it was obvious to her that it was a masquerade required by the circumstances. I was aware of her approach, which is why I said nothing to her about my decision to be baptized in France and to become a Christian.

Every time I crossed myself, I noticed my relations' disconcertment and the expressions on their faces made it obvious to me that I had managed to cause them profound discomfort. I don't remember them saying anything about it, but it was clear to me that they had been advised by my uncle not to make an issue of it and to let time take its toll. In hindsight, I can say that it was a fascinating exercise in psychology. On her own, Aunt Hilda would probably have been unable to overcome the shock I had caused her, but the self-control demonstrated by my uncle was impressive and I am grateful to both of them, though especially to him, for behaving so wisely. Had they behaved differently, I would have stood my ground and gone ahead with an act from which there might have been no turning back. I would have left their home without reserve. At that time, I was quite mature and independent and had no fear whatsoever of running away from home. I had thought about it often during my first few months in France, each time deciding to postpone my implementation of the idea. It was at that time that I started corresponding with my grandmother, who was now living in Jerusalem. We corresponded in German and I used to begin my letters with the words, *"Meine teuere omama,"* which means "My very dearest grandmother," even though I didn't remember her. She was, after all, my mother's mother and that, as far as I was concerned, made her someone close.

Parallel to all these events, Aunt Hilda registered me for the final year in elementary school. According to the French school system at that time, children completed five years of elementary school before moving on to a high school for a further seven years, after which they earned their school leaving certificate. Since I had arrived in France in April 1946 and I was 11 years old, I was accepted into the final term of the last year at elementary school. On my first day at school, the teacher dictated a few lines to the pupils. After checking the results, she decided to summon my aunt and told her that in all her years as a teacher (she was about 55) she had never seen such an abundance of spelling mistakes in a single piece of writing by a boy of my age. She added that it might be necessary for me to leave the class.

My aunt exerted some heavy pressure on the system and I remained in the class until the end of the school year. I failed the high school entrance exams miserably and it was decided to keep me back a year. I was 11-and-a-half years old by then and my classmates were ten. I was taller than them all and had led a life that was full of rich and varied experiences and memories; I was also the weakest pupil in the class. Although I improved with time, mainly through the help of my aunt's private tutoring, I developed a lack of confidence in school and this troubled me. I hated school and often reacted violently. But my teacher, who knew about my past, handled me with kid gloves. Whenever necessary, she explained to me patiently how I was supposed to behave. She forgave me for most of the unacceptable things I did and she really was a wonderful educator.

At home, too, I envied Annette, who was such a successful girl. Sometimes, I even treated her violently. Once, when Annette and I were 12, my uncle and aunt decided to go out for the evening and left the two of us at home alone. I remember immediately going into her room and beating her. I don't remember the reason and I am not sure if even there was one. As luck would have it, my uncle and aunt had forgotten to take something with them and quickly returned home. They were horrified by what they saw and decided not to go out that night. It was not the first time I had acted violently at home.

On another occasion, I broke the glass panel in the door that separated the waiting room of my uncle's veterinary clinic and the family's living quarters. The outburst came as a result of my uncle's request that I refrain from passing through the waiting room when it was full of his patients and their owners. It was an inviolable house rule and I saw it as restricting my freedom; it antagonized me to such an extent that as soon as the waiting room was full of patients, I drove my fist through the colored glass. I broke the glass and also injured myself. Again, I had caused a rumpus and this time my aunt feared the reaction of my uncle, who was about to return from doing his rounds on the farms. She waited for him by the entrance to the clinic and before he called in the first patient, she told him what had happened and asked that he be gentle with me. And so it was. They explained to me with infinite wisdom and understanding that nothing can justify such behavior and I, of course, agreed with them. I knew I had been out of line but how could I explain to those nice people how hard it often was for me to overcome the extreme envy I had accumulated within me that sometimes turned into sheer hatred towards everyone and towards myself.

Aunt Hilda was summoned to the principal's office during the third school term of 1947. I was also present at that meeting. The principal explained to my aunt that I was too old to be admitted into an academic high school and proposed I continue my studies in a vocational high school. He said this in a quite dry, somewhat official and authoritative tone. My aunt was horrified, probably more from the tone of voice than from the content. She expressed her shock at the uncompromising attitude of the school system and explained to the principal that I was a victim of the war and that I was undergoing a process of rehabilitation. She added that the principal's demand would sabotage any chance of my being reformed. Apart from this, she was horrified and most saddened to learn that in a vocational high school I would not be able to learn Latin.

It is quite possible that this matter raised a small smile to the principal's pursed lips, but the atmosphere was harsh and he remained official and patronizing, with a stern expression on his face. The conversation lasted quite a long time and my aunt fought bravely on behalf of absolute justice. Finally, the principal agreed to see what he could do and said he would let us know his decision. As we exited the principal's office, my aunt continued to complain that the decision might prevent me from studying Latin, a language that, in my aunt's eyes, was the pinnacle of learning and one to which every Polish Jewish intellectual aspired. This attitude was still alive and kicking even at a period when the Latin language had lost much of its importance and was no longer essential to any kind of breakthrough. There was no reference to the fact that there was something here of much greater significance to me, because I was now facing a choice of continuing my schooling in an official and serious capacity with a chance of achieving matriculation level and going on to university, or learning a skill and stopping there.

A few days later, we received a reply from the school, saying that due to my special situation and because I was a victim of the war, the official committee had decided to allow me to continue my studies in the town's high school. I remember well the outburst of joy among my new family. Their obvious concern for me touched my heart and drew me closer to them. Until that moment, I had made great efforts not to like them, as this would have been interpreted in my eyes as a betrayal to my parents and Aunt Angele, which was nothing new for me. When my parents disappeared and I still didn't know for sure that they were in German hands, I rejected all emotional connection with anyone else. For a long time, I waged a struggle against my feelings so as not to become close to Aunt Angele. Even when this fight had dissipated, I remained aloof from all emotional involvement. It was my way of preserving my parents' memory and I was convinced it was the only right way to respect it.

There were occasions when I was on the verge of breaking, like that time during the war, when I ran for my life from the lady in the church, in order to avoid temptation. Only after the war, when I was still full of hopes of my parents returning after all, did I manage to soften a little. I developed fond feelings towards Aunt Angele and started to feel good in her home. It was the way I always behaved when faced with a new environment — building inaccessible emotional buttresses against it. So my beginnings in France were difficult and complex, both because of the warm family framework in which I found no place for myself and refused to integrate into and because of the troubles I had in school.

As for wanting to be baptized, I repeated my request several times during my first few months in France. Uncle Milek continued to say that there was no problem with it but that it was better at that moment to focus on more important things and those which demanded immediate attention. He promised that my wish would be dealt with later, but at some point, I stopped crossing myself. Years later, Uncle Milek told me that from my behavior he had noticed a change in my agenda. In 1947, my aunt and uncle sent me to be taught Hebrew by a teacher in the local Jewish community and shortly afterwards, I began studying with the local rabbi in preparation from my *Bar Mitzvah*, which was due to take place in March 1948.

With his wise and gentle approach, my Uncle Milek succeeded in modifying my powerful need to volunteer to help the needy of the world that had filled me when I first arrived in their home. With no argument or attempts to dissuade me, he was able to counter my plans. The matter was never even mentioned in our conversations. He was simply aware of the changes I had undergone over time in my new life, changes that brought with them a transformation in my priorities without my even noticing it. Later, after discussing the matter, I couldn't help but marvel at the psychological insights and emotional wisdom of this modest man, as well as his sangfroid.

Thanks to my wonderful elementary school teacher, Ms. David, a mature woman with a heart of gold, as gentle as she was considerate, I managed to improve my grades a little. As a result, I was ultimately able to get into high school, albeit late, but I did it. However, I was once again in trouble during my first year at high school in late 1947, early 1948. My classmates knew that I was a foreigner but they didn't harass me much. There was the occasional outburst of giggling when I was called to the board, but this happened to many others, too. Perhaps my accent was still a bit different or I sounded hesitant and unsure of myself. For one reason or another, some of the kids used to laugh at me behind my back. At one recess, a blond-haired boy with an impish face who was in the same class as me accosted me and said something about Jews. I don't remember exactly what he said but whatever it was, it sounded insulting. My reaction was immediate and very violent. I gave him a cruel beating, thinking nothing of where I was or the people around me. The other kids must have been afraid to pull us apart and the boy got a thorough thrashing. Within less than a minute a discipline counselor — a mandatory post in French high schools at that time — arrived on the scene and led me straight to his office. He reprimanded me, threatened to send me to the principal's office and added that I might not be allowed to continue my studies at that school.

Again, my aunt was summoned to the school, this time to meet the deputy principal, who was responsible for administration and discipline. I was invited to be present at the meeting. He looked frightening — a big, heavy-set man, with a red face and small eyes that were hidden behind his puffed-out cheeks. He asked me to tell him what had happened. It transpired that the parents of the boy I had beaten had made an official complaint against me. My aunt appeared helpless and confused. At the deputy principal's request I explained what had happened, how it had all begun. I quoted what the boy had said about my Jewishness and relayed how much that had hurt me. I must have sounded truthful and sensed that the frightening heavy-set man had softened his attitude and sympathized with what I was feeling. I even noticed a small smile at the corner of his mouth as I tried to explain the reason for my actions. He, of course, said the kinds of things he was obliged to say: that violence was unacceptable, that it was better to discuss things even when there are large differences of opinion, that a person has to learn to control himself, etc. I relaxed because I could see that inside that oversized body there was hidden a good soul. It was agreed that I would stay on at school, but at that stage, only on the condition and in the hope that an incident of this kind would not be repeated.

As we walked out of the school my aunt scolded me for my irresponsible behavior. I was annoyed by what she said; she knew that the boy had said something that hurt me deeply, but she would have preferred for me not to respond. To me, this attitude seemed terrible. I had expected her to support me, to justify my act, but she did the absolute opposite. I was disappointed and hurt. That evening, Aunt Hilda told Uncle Milek, in my presence, what had happened that day in school. I got the impression that my uncle was not shocked by my reaction. He looked at me fondly and told me to try to avoid lashing out. He explained to me gravely that I could get into trouble and that it could be dangerous to hit someone, but he didn't reproach me and I felt that this time, at least, I had come out on top.

The deputy principal was the father of two kids who also attended the school. During my years there I became friendly with them and often visited them at their home, which was located in one of the buildings within the school grounds. It was a handsome official residence reserved for members of the school staff and I sometimes met their father there. He always smiled at me in a very friendly manner. In the end, the parents of the boy I had beaten up dropped their complaint against me and our relationship returned to normal. I felt that a change had taken place in my status among my schoolmates. It seemed to have become clear to everyone that although I wasn't brilliant academically, I was not to be despised. The incident, no doubt, raised my self-esteem and improved my feeling in the classroom and in school generally. In 1948 or 1949, as my grades gradually improved and I became an average student, I managed to rid myself more or less of my complex of being a weak student. I no longer felt inferior in most of the subjects and was able to compare myself to the other students.

As my school life improved, my ties to Christianity loosened, I no longer felt Austrian and even my emotional ties with Belgium faded. In France, I was awarded the status of "undetermined [indéterminé] citizenship" and due to this special civilian status I was required to report to the police once a month. The police officers were not particularly pleasant and their attitude did not contribute to my positive feelings towards France at that time and didn't turn me into much of a Francophile. I didn't really feel French, so I remained with my Judaism. I became committed to the community and it was this that gave me the sense of belonging that France did not. My *Bar Mitzvah* ceremony also left its mark on my identity. I started to feel very Jewish and began to put on phylacteries every day, a custom that was supposed to distinguish me from all my French friends. I was not devout and, in fact, I was not religious, but I wanted to signal to myself that I had something of my own, and that this something is what sets me apart from the environment in which I live.

My *Bar Mitzvah* ceremony was an important milestone in my life. It appeared that everybody in the community knew all about me, so that many of them participated in my celebration, which was quite unusual, at least according to what my uncle and aunt told me later. The community's cantor prepared me for prayer and made sure to conduct the ceremony in an especially festive manner. Our guests were dressed elegantly and I could feel the warmth and love being lavished upon me by all those present. My uncle and aunt were very emotional and the ceremony constituted something of a demonstration of sympathy towards me and, especially, towards Hilda and Milek, who had taken in a lost child and raised him to such a dignified position. I no longer had the clear voice of a church choirboy; it was still a soprano voice, and apparently had a nice tone to it but, as happens in adolescence, it had a tendency to slip into a lower tone. The occasion, being called to the Torah and reading from the weekly portion with the congregation listening to me with baited breath brought back memories from a different world.

The *Bar Mitzvah* ceremony, with all the preparations and emotions it engendered, along with the intimate meeting with Judaism, was a turning point in my life that was followed by a good period for me. For the first time in years, I felt an inner completeness that allowed me to move away from myself and to make time for real things. The ceremony had placed me center stage of my town's Jewish community and, as a result, I stopped feeling alien there and enjoyed being identified with a well-known and respectable family. I was proud of being a part of this family that enjoyed the respect of the community for its contribution and, in no small measure, for the fact that they had adopted me during the difficult post-war period, a period that was hard on everybody, especially from a financial point of view. In time, Annette and I became very close and regarded each other as brother and sister. We had become a family unit in every sense, a family that provided much support and a sense of belonging.

My schoolmates often spoke about their families, their parents, their brothers or sisters and their way of life. They spoke glowingly and with pride about how they spent their weekends, often competing with and trying to impress their friends or relatives with stories of their interesting and sometimes outrageous outings. At first, I tended to avoid these conversations. My friends talked among themselves about their plans, intentions or wishes. When I first arrived at the school in France, these conversations all appeared quite silly to me and I never succeeded to involve myself in them. It was hard for me to share things about my new family and I was unable to share with others any details concerning my plans, since I had no plans for the future. However, a change took place in me shortly before my *Bar Mitzvah*.

The awareness of the family issue, and the feeling that I now belonged to a normal family and the satisfaction I drew from this, must have freed some of the constraints that imprisoned my heart and resulted in my often being included in conversations based on confidences and closeness. Of course, at first, none of my friends sensed that I was investing considerable efforts in this move, nor did they notice that I was gradually opening up to things and people; no one paid any attention to the slow process of change I was undergoing — a process of healing and emotional integration in my day-to-day life, which was all the result of the new behavior I had deliberately imposed upon myself.

At the same time, I came to the conclusion that, ultimately, life had been good to me and that I was fortunate. I had a family I could be proud of, we had a life of our own and I even had something I could talk about with my friends. I started to describe events and adventures that had or had not happened. I daresay my friends also exaggerated sometimes and set free their imaginations, but that was of little importance so long as I could talk, could enter the circle of conversation, could be part of society and could live in accordance with the norms acceptable to children and young people in general. I gradually opened myself to the kind of chitchat or small talk that, until then, I had found either dangerous or unsuitable for me. And I found it delightful. It was the best possible tool for discovering my place in the new environment in which I was living. Gradually, I began to discover a thing or two, here and there, about my new family and about myself, and I became quite an outgoing boy. Of course, the decision to become like this was forced, but with time it became second nature and after this big change, I began to feel surer of myself in company and more secure.

At around this time there was another slight falling out with my aunt. One day, an acquaintance of Aunt Hilda, whom I had never met before, came to visit. They sat next to me in the living room, talking about this and that. Suddenly, I don't remember in what context, my aunt told her guest that we were of Jewish extraction.

This expression riled me and I interrupted her with a rudeness that was totally unacceptable, saying in a very commanding voice that we were not of Jewish extraction, we were Jews. My tone must have sounded very impertinent indeed and I was immediately reproached. I clearly recall the woman's acute embarrassment at finding herself suddenly in the midst of a dispute between my aunt and I, and me being highly agitated and unable to control my feelings. In front of her guest, I accused Aunt Hilda of being ashamed of her Jewishness, which, as far as I was concerned, was the only source of pride I had in this country, and other things in this vein.

To me, the euphemistic style of conversation, the discomfort vis-à-vis Judaism, the desire to prove to French people that to be French was the pinnacle of all aspirations, were all totally unacceptable. This was typical behavior of those refugees from Poland who had come to France during the pre-war years, or shortly after World War II. They felt they had to be grateful to their hosts for having a country and for giving Jews equal rights there. The inferiority complex of those Eastern European Jews was even expressed in their sycophantic attitude towards the French Jews. And indeed, these veteran Jews, especially those who had come from the Alsace district, looked down on the newcomers and their alienation was sometimes even more intense than that of the French non-Jews.

Even then, I couldn't accept this kind of behavior, which I saw as shameful. Although I was gradually beginning to feel comfortable in France, I was always very much aware of where I belonged. Not only had I never seen my Jewishness as a burden or a problem; on the contrary, at long last, I was finally a Jew, after all those years of being forced to hide the fact. I have never understood the source of the reservation so typical of some of my Jewish acquaintances. The war was over and I was now living under my own national identity; what was the point of all those airs and graces that seemed to me so tasteless and obsequious?

I often argued over this issue with Aunt Hilda, especially when we were out walking the dog in the evenings, as we did two or three times a week. We spoke a lot on these occasions and there was a relaxed and very open atmosphere between us. By this time, I was already feeling very close to her and Uncle Milek. They behaved towards me as parents should behave towards their children and as they behaved towards their daughter, Annette, and hence, they had become very dear to me. On our walks together, we tried to understand what had happened to make her and me so different from each other with regard to our Jewishness.

Aunt Hilda had been raised and educated in Galicia after World War I, in other words, in the district belonging to Poland. Her indigenous environment had been both Jewish and Polish. Growing up in a well-off family with three older brothers who protected her, she didn't particularly suffer from being a Jew. After completing her education she met the love of her life and went with him to Africa, after which they moved to France. Although for a part of the war she and her daughter had been obliged to go into hiding, they returned immediately afterwards to their previous residence and easily reintegrated into local life. The family that remained in Poland perished in the Holocaust. After the war, she had a strong affinity to France, as well as a feeling of belonging to the town in which she lived. She established a good circle of friends in the town, both Jews and non-Jews.

My aunt was a lively conversationalist, full of *joie de vivre* and was an active and valued member of the local Jewish community. She suffered deeply from the unaccommodating attitude of the veteran French Jews who refused to fully accept the Polish Jews, often referring to them as refugees and thus insulting their status and their honor. My Aunt Hilda did her best to be accepted into French society, or at least into French Jewish society. She was very honest about her Jewishness, but it was more emotional than religious. The High Holidays reminded her of her childhood home and she celebrated them with all the traditional dishes and created the right atmosphere. In her Judaism there was much nostalgia and yearning for her lost family. In a certain sense she was even a religious Jew, but her belief was superficial and non-committal. Although she attended the synagogue on some of the holy days and even joined in the prayers, on these visits, too, the social aspect was no less important than the religious. Like other women of her standing in the community, she also considered synagogue attendance to be a respectable and enjoyable way of spending time, a sociable meeting of friends, as well as a chance to clear one's soul. I would never, of course, misinterpret the fact that my aunt's synagogue attendance, surrounded by her fellow religionists, provided her with a kind of warm nest and took her, full of yearning, back to the town of her birth and the home of her parents. It was certainly pleasant. Thus was the Jewishness of my Aunt Hilda: warm, nostalgic and embracing.

For me, Judaism was war — an endless struggle, harsh confrontations, constant questions and a never-ending search for answers. Even though I was not a devout Jew, Judaism was the focal point of my life. My connection to my Jewishness developed gradually out of suffering and a desire to move away from it, and it evolved into a source of fulfillment. Because of my Jewishness, in my childhood I had become a Christian. It had led me to losing my family. Those painful childhood years were the result of my being Jewish. For many years, it constituted an obstacle to a normal life and even if I had been able to discard it, it would not have made a difference to the end result. My fate was cast. I was a Jew and that was that. All that was left for me to do was to learn to live with it. But gradually, in a way almost dictated by nature, my Jewishness became the essence of my life. My aunt, on the other hand, could take a step back from it and casually say, "We are of Jewish extraction." For me, this offhanded sentence and all it signified came as a deep shock. Already then, the basic Jewishness within me was a major part of my identity, which had not yet been sufficiently formed.

The conversations during our evening walks inevitably reached a painful point: "Henri, I am worried about you. Although lately you have been quiet and calm, when it comes to the Jewish issue you are truly fanatical and are showing signs of aggression. You have to relax; otherwise you're going to suffer for it." Hilda already had some bitter experiences with me over this, including the trouble I had got into at school. But that belonged to another time, since my behavior had improved immeasurably. "You really do cause a lot of trouble," she went on relentlessly, "and your uncle and I are very worried about you. We don't know what to do to soften your attitude to the subject." It was never an easy conversation for me, because I knew how much they cared for me and for my future. On the Jewish issue, I was torn between two conflicting feelings. On the one hand, I didn't know how to explain to them that I was unable to "soften" my position; on the other, I loved them very much and the thought that I was hurting them unnecessarily was unbearable. How interesting, therefore, that just a few years earlier, the same Aunt Hilda had been so concerned about the possibility of the Jewish nation losing one of its sons to Christianity. And now, here she was feeling that it was her job to restrain my Jewishness.

In both instances, I succeeded in shocking her. She would often tell me, with considerable insight, that I was far too extreme and that if I didn't wish to suffer in life I would have to adopt a more flexible attitude. These arguments took place when I was about 14 years old and continued until I was 18. But, I gradually became too busy to discuss such weighty subjects, since the local Jewish community was developing some attractive activities for young people and like others of my age, I was also busy with my schoolwork.

In 1949, my grandmother suddenly announced that she was planning to pay us a visit on her way from Israel to the United States. She had decided to spend some time with us in order to ensure that Aunt Hilda and Uncle Milek were taking suitable care of me. I was curious to meet my grandmother and was pleased by the prospect of her arrival. The days leading to her visit were filled with excitement and expectations. The term "grandmother" was not familiar to me; it had no emotional connotations for me. I didn't remember her from my childhood, since she had left Vienna when I was three years old. As the day of her arrival drew nearer, I decided to delve deeper into who she was; the idea that I was about to meet someone who was so close to my mother gave me no rest and the weeks were nerve-wracking for me. For days and nights my mind was engaged by the thought that a new person was about to enter my life. Having seen no pictures of her, I tried to imagine her resembling my mother, whose face I remembered well. I don't remember if I already had any pictures of my parents by then.

Around that time, several family photographs had arrived, mostly from Mr. Hourmont. They were photographs that my parents had apparently left with him for safekeeping. I had had no pictures of my family whilst staying with Aunt Angele, and I was often troubled by this fact, worried I'd be unable to remember what my parents, Aunt Hanna'le and Uncle Salo looked like. I didn't want to forget their faces. In time, the fear turned into anxiety and the anxiety became a nightmare: Here, I had parents but I can barely remember the silhouettes of their faces and the shadows of their bodies. Their actual faces evaded me, fading away and disappearing gradually. Those were the traumatic thoughts that I sometimes had at night, and which is probably why I was so occupied with what my grandmother looked like.

I was hoping to find some resemblance to my mother in that grandmother, who was still a faceless person as far as I was concerned, an abstract figure just beginning to materialize even before I had met her. But I was not the only one concerned with the visit of Grandmother Yocheved. Hilda and Milek were also quite troubled by it. They knew that the object of her visit was to check that they were raising me as they had promised and were afraid that she might change her mind if she was not satisfied with their treatment of me and would send me to live elsewhere. They were well aware that one was not allowed to appeal against Grandmother Yocheved's decisions and they were apprehensive about the visit. The stress level rose as "Judgment Day" approached. And then, Grandmother Yocheved arrived, in all her glory.

Grandmother Yocheved, Haifa 1949.

My grandmother was a short woman with broad shoulders and a straight back. She was still handsome to look at and had obviously been very attractive as a young woman. Her look was alert and inquisitive, her small eyes darting quickly from side to side and settling on everything in her vicinity, as if she was all-seeing and nothing escaped her eagle eye. So sharply alert was she that I noticed how people conversing with her immediately adopted a defensive stance. If she looked at you, you straightaway felt uncomfortable. Her authoritativeness undermined most people's self-confidence. Her vitality and command burst out of her body with a power that was incredible. No one could ignore her presence. Nonetheless, she was also feminine and loving. As soon as she saw me for the first time, she was filled with maternal tenderness, which somewhat softened her frightening first impression. Her presence terrified Aunt Hilda, who did everything she could to appease her, in the hope of passing the test and being allowed to keep me with her.

Grandmother examined the quality of the food I was being fed. She would lift the lid off Aunt Hilda's cooking pots to scrutinize their contents. It didn't take her long to assume control of the kitchen and then it was she who cooked all our meals. Everyone surrendered to her demands. She really was a strong woman with leadership qualities. We often went for walks around the town, just the two of us, and we talked about all kinds of things. I enjoyed those times, but I sought my mother in her and didn't find her. They were so unalike. I was quite disappointed that the connection I had hoped to achieve with my mother by means of my grandmother did not, in the end, materialize.

After staying with us for a month, Grandmother left for New York. She seemed quite pleased with what she had seen and that her grandson, the son of her only daughter, was receiving a European education, something she regarded as of supreme importance. I never saw her again. We corresponded regularly and we knew everything about each other, but there were no further meetings. The memories from this visit were carved in my Aunt Hilda's heart as a horrible experience. Years later, she would relive the terror that gripped her whenever Grandmother Yocheved lifted one of her pot lids or made some comment or other; and the suspense that she withstood while waiting for the final decision on my future. She felt enormous relief when it was decided that I would remain with them and there wasn't a happier woman in the whole world than she. Often, she would emotionally reconstruct those moments and I knew then how much she loved me and how dear I was to her.

One day, when I was 15 years old, my mother's brother Latzo from New York arrived suddenly in France. He was apparently on a business trip to Europe and had decided to visit us; his behavior led us to believe that he was on a mission on behalf of my grandmother, who was already living in New York at the time. He turned out to be a very friendly man, warm and family oriented. He brought a lot of gifts for the family and for me, and he stayed with us for a few days before returning home. His pleasantness totally dispersed the clouds of concern aroused by his sudden appearance in our home. Uncle Latzo's visit was a great deal friendlier than that of Grandmother Yocheved. My grandmother had assumed full control of the home of Uncle Milek and Aunt Hilda and had behaved like a tyrannical queen, whereas Latzo was a charming and modest guest, who had done his best not to impose himself on his hosts by changing their daily routine.

By that time, I was already feeling calmer and more relaxed. I felt at ease with my family, I was more or less integrated into local society and conducted myself like any other boy my age. Nonetheless, every visit by one of my relatives took me back to my past. There was a strong resemblance between Latzo and his brother Salo and although I thoroughly enjoyed Uncle Latzo's visit, I found this similarity quite disconcerting. When we talked, in German, of course, as I had done with Salo, I was transported back several years to the embrace of the people who had been so very dear to me. I found myself in a kind of whirlwind that pulled me down into those depths from which I had labored so hard to rise back to ground level. He had the same physical appearance, the same glance, the same soft voice and, especially, the same smile. In fact, I was divided yet again between two totally conflicting desires. On the one hand, his presence made me happy; I felt wonderful in his company and I wanted to take him with me on a journey back in time. I was connected to my past and it would often pop up with no prior warning. This time, I wanted Uncle Latzo with me on that difficult but pleasant journey. On the other hand, his presence opened a wound that I believed I had managed to close, even to heal; yet the scab that had formed over it was thin and fragile and easily cracked. The jerk from my present to my past could be confusing at times. Aunt Hilda and Uncle Milek knew nothing of my feelings, as I had been accustomed since early childhood not to share my thoughts and feelings with anyone and no one else was party to the storm that raged in my heart and in my mind. Despite all the thoughts and reservations that accompanied Latzo's visit, I was ultimately very pleased that it had taken place and that I had had the chance to meet my uncle.

My life in my uncles' home in France continued to be pleasant and well balanced. My daily schedule was like that of any other boy my age — I went to high school, had lots of friends and belonged to the Scout movement; I did plenty of sport, especially basketball and cycling. My relations with my aunt and uncle were very good and I felt good in their company. However, strange ideas were racing around my brain and disturbing my peace. Unlike a regular boy who lives with his parents and is an integral part of his family, I always remained someone on the sidelines, looking in. Although I was accepted into this place and into this family, who treated me as their son in every way, and even though this family really was my family, I still never felt that I completely belonged there. It was probably my own fault for nurturing this feeling of alienation. The family had welcomed me with warmth and love and had never intended for me to feel like an outsider, but this was my feeling and it remained harsh. I dwelt on it a lot, analyzing every situation; every incident at home was interpreted against a background of this feeling. Possibly, this is natural for a boy to harbor such feelings — a boy who had nothing and has suddenly been integrated into a loving family feels the need to be eternally grateful for all they are doing for him. A boy who lives with his real parents is not grateful; he simply takes everything for granted, whereas I took nothing for granted.

I had arrived at their home empty-handed, with a heart devoid of love, and the feeling that I was indebted weighed very heavily on me. I was constantly afraid that I was not behaving properly, that I might be a disappointment to them, that I presented a financial burden and other thoughts and reflections of this kind. These feelings were constant and I found them hard to bear. I also felt guilty for thinking that I was unable to accept them as fully as they accepted me. I understood that they deserved more than I was able to give them and this intensified the weight of my guilt. An example of this is the postcard I wrote to Aunt Hilda in honor of some event that took place about a year after my arrival in her home.

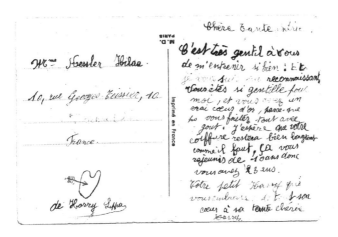

A postcard, written in French, which I sent to Aunt Hilda.

*To my dear and beloved aunt,*

*It is very nice of you to take such good care of me. I am extremely grateful to you for this and you really do have a heart of gold and everything you do is in such good taste. I hope your hairstyle lasts for a long time because it makes you look ten years younger…*

*To [my] beloved aunt, from your little Harry, who kisses you with all his heart.*

For many years I went back to reread this postcard and, even to this day, it unsettles me. It serves as, ostensibly, naïve testimony to the feeling of guilt that accompanied me throughout the years I spent with my uncle and aunt in France. I know that there is no room here for anger or resentment. Aunt Hilda and Uncle Milek were wonderful people. I was attached to them like a son to his biological parents, even more so, since this love was tempered by genuine respect for everything they did for me, under circumstances that were not at all easy. But it was here that the difficulty lay; I was unable to accept their bounty. Indeed, I wasn't hypocritical nor was I sanctimonious; I was merely a boy who found it hard to reciprocate expressions of love unconditionally, as it should be in a family.

Within the family, I was referred to jokingly as "Jesuit." The Jesuits are an ancient fundamentalist Christian order established in the sixteenth century. In time, the cult members were tarnished with the negative connotations of hypocrisy, sanctimony and sycophancy. Although I was given the nickname in jest, it was not entirely without basis. There was also something about the atmosphere in the house that could have been the result of internal emotional pressure, but I felt driven to exaggerated expressions of bonhomie, especially towards Aunt Hilda, although it might also have been because of her own personality. Aunt Hilda was the pampered daughter of a wealthy Polish Jewish family and, in spite of the modest lifestyle in her French home during the early post-war years, she sometimes continued to behave as if she were still that spoilt little girl who constantly expected to be the center of attention. I interpreted her behavior as an inherent need for flattery. Uncle Milek and Annette never behaved like this and even embarrassed her at times by commenting on her behavior. I, on the other hand, heaped endless compliments and thanks on her, which might just have been my own need to please or, at the same time, a "masculine" kind of maturity that, even at an early age, had been part of my personality. Since I had been accustomed from early childhood to hide my real feelings, it just came naturally to me.

Ever since my "confessions" in the church confessional in Brussels, I hadn't confessed anything to anyone. I had never poured out my heart to anyone, nor had I ever consulted with another person.

Of course, I refer to genuine confession and consultation of the kind that are real and come from deep within, not the confessions I would "fabricate" for the priest. Masquerading, pretending, playacting — all these were formerly the protective tools I used against the enemy and, as I have already shown, they came to me easily, except that this time, I exercised these tools on people who loved me. Perhaps these traits can all be examined from an additional angle. Perhaps this was what I chose so as to maintain my real "me." I set my own boundaries and drafted them in several ways.

Our social life in the city was conducted within a small and intimate circle of friends. My uncle and aunt's friends were good people — mostly Jews who had left antisemitic Poland before the war and had come to live in France, where they could obtain a university education. They had careers as engineers, chemists and physicians, etc., belonged to the upper-middle class, made good incomes and enjoyed a pleasant quality of life. When they met, they spoke French as well as quite a lot of Polish, especially among the women. It was a bourgeois, rather conservative group that maintained a form of Jewish tradition that was mostly based on nostalgia. They felt very good in France and a large majority of them subsequently remained in France.

Their get-togethers usually took place on Sundays. They took turns hosting and we children enjoyed playing together, although I never formed a real connection with any of them. I became very fond of Hilda and Milek's friends and I maintained contact with some of them even after I left the town. Nonetheless, I didn't particularly respect them because they seemed indifferent to their environment and, in many ways, detached from it. They were like everyone else, but their roots laid elsewhere and this, they chose to forget. I often got the impression that they lived neither here nor there. They were people whose lives were dictated by circumstances. In my eyes, this behavior lacked self-respect. The only one who had the ability and the drive to navigate his life in accordance with the path he had chosen for himself and to influence his fate was Uncle Milek. I had a great deal of respect for him, but ultimately, he, too, surrendered to the gray reality of his life and became a victim of the day-to-day drudgery that occupied him at the expense of everything else. He was the only man I knew at that time who had a defiant, perhaps even revolutionary, spark; he didn't accept his destiny as something to be taken for granted.

I have already described his struggle with the Polish Army, which was not conducted as some patriotic urge or out of any other higher motive, rather from a willingness to swim against the current and to "show the gentiles" what he was made of. However, in the end, even this courageous rebel became exhausted and he opted for a quiet life. Uncle Milek was a man whose life had known many upheavals during a period of serious unrest, and his quest for a "normal" existence was something he took for granted. Thus, I do not judge him for his values. His willingness to accept me into his family under those circumstances was in itself testimony to the magnanimity of this man. After that, he gave in and lived his life like everyone else.

Like most children, I was sensitive to injustice, and during my years in Belgium I had been exposed to many such instances. I had watched with my own eyes as German soldiers forcibly dragged away Jewish adults and children. I was always infuriated by the fact that we were unable to live as we wished, but were forced to hide, to conceal our identity and to exist in constant fear. I saw bombings in which simple, innocent and pure-hearted people were killed; as a relatively small child I was witness to sights of extreme violence. I saw things that were hard to bear. I have no doubt that this cumulative experience, as I knew it, had ramifications that later influenced the development of my personality in ways that were not always evident or explicable. For as long as I can remember, injustice was something I could not stomach.

During my childhood in Belgium, I used to bury these feelings deep within me and I prevented myself from even slightly uncovering them. I was an observer on the sidelines, never mixing in since I knew that I had to protect myself against any response that could put my life in danger. The efforts demanded of me were superhuman. Usually, I held myself back and was later angry for not having had the necessary courage to reveal my true self. But deep inside, I knew I had done the right thing. I learned to live in peace with this behavior of mine. I became accustomed to thinking first and foremost of myself; I reacted with sangfroid and always checked to see how I could remove myself from an awkward situation unscathed.

After the war, when survival was no longer an issue, I gradually returned to my true self and allowed myself to react more naturally to things, in accordance with my values and my moods. I was no longer required to practice self-control and could act and respond as I wished. I recall quite a few instances at school in France when I acted fiercely in defense of a fellow student who had become the victim of some injustice on the part of a teacher or the establishment. By then, I was already feeling stronger. I no longer feared expulsion from school, I wasn't afraid of the establishment and, especially, there was no need to feel that my life was in danger. I often exaggerated in my war for "justice," and more than once my behavior resulted in unnecessary complications.

I recall well one such occasion when I was 15 or 16 years old; a teacher ordered a student to leave the classroom in the middle of a written exam because he suspected that the student was copying a note that lay on his desk. It happened right next to me and I had seen the note being placed there by the student next to him, who had received it from another desk. The accused student had not even read the note, but the teacher insisted that he had copied from it and declared him guilty of cheating. The boy next to him, who was the guilty party, kept quiet, did not confess and let the teacher blame and punish his innocent classmate. This infuriated me. I stood up, pointed to the real culprit and came to the defense of the victim. The teacher didn't like my interference, said I was being insolent and made it known to everyone present that he would "deal" with me after the exam. In the end, it was I who was reprimanded. Moreover, the boy who had cheated was annoyed with me, while the boy who was about to be unjustly punished barely thanked me for my intervention. For me, it was an important, albeit not particularly helpful, lesson.

Throughout the years of my youth, I got mixed up in several other such instances. On another occasion, I came to the defense of a friend in summer school. One of the instructors beat him as he was standing next to me and I immediately set about fighting this instructor as he turned out to be a violent and wicked character. He tried hard to get me expelled from the summer school, but didn't succeed. In this case, I, as well as other boys, was able to persuade the school's administration that this man had a negative influence and he was fired from his job.

I shall dwell for a while on a brief period when I was in my teens that seemed to have some impact on my future, although at the time it appeared no more than a passing episode. I was 17 years old when a group of youngsters from the local Jewish community, myself included, got together to establish a youth club with a focus on activity connected with being Jewish. Most of the youths who joined our club were not particularly religious, but felt the need to belong to some framework that had a common denominator for all of us: our Jewishness. Our parents were mostly of Polish origin, who had escaped to France and were still firmly rooted in their Jewishness, whereas we — kids who were my age or a little older — felt that our Jewish roots were weakening as our ties to France were growing stronger and becoming second nature to us. We felt we had to do something in order to connect to our unique identity. So, for the first time, I found myself involved in an activity that did not touch on my own agenda and pleasures, and I felt quite pleased with myself.

We established the club and forged ties with the Jewish communities in two additional towns in the region. In time, we turned into a large group, held social meetings and discussed issues that were connected to our lives and future in France. However, it soon became apparent that these issues were not sufficiently attractive to tempt youngsters to join, especially as the established Zionist youth movements in the two other towns had more to offer than we did. We realized eventually that there was no point in continuing. Hence, we shifted our focus to dance parties, table tennis contests and other enjoyable activities, which provided a suitable framework for Jewish youngsters of both sexes to meet and socialize. Girls and boys met each other there, became couples, married and established traditional Jewish families in their hometowns. In time, some of the young people left the town to continue their studies in far off universities; others left when they were drafted into the French Army and participated in the Algerian war, and our organization, which had been so full of good intentions, reached the end of its road.

Even though the activities within this framework lacked clear definition or objective, they still managed to consolidate the local youngsters around a common denominator — we were all Jews. As for me, being a part of this group might have helped pave the way to an additional feeling of Jewish belonging. I should point out that I was the only Holocaust survivor in this group. Most of the members had been born locally, had gone into hiding with their parents in farms and villages in France and had managed somehow to survive. They saw themselves as French Jews. I felt wonderful among these young people; I was absolutely one of them and was quite active. I felt the warmth of the group and wondered at the idea of my belonging to this large family that sometimes detached itself from day-to-day affairs and devoted its thoughts and energies to an objective that was beyond the routine life of youngsters our age. Through this activity I was able, in a way, to connect with my past and I often thought that my parents would certainly be pleased to know that I had returned to my roots. Although this chapter in my teen years lasted only for only a brief period of time, it seems to me, in retrospect, that it opened a new path for me, one that navigated my way for the future — the need to belong to something with Jewish ideals that was more than family.

Still, I felt smothered, despite the pleasant family life I enjoyed in France. I felt good with my family, even though I was immersed in a kind of disquiet, a stifling feeling that never dissipated. Sometimes my thoughts would wander. I saw myself in far-off lands and on my own. When my uncle and aunt went on their annual vacation in August with their daughter Annette, I managed to wriggle out of going with them in order to join Scout summer camps, at first as a regular member and later as a counselor. With all my love for my aunt and uncle, I sometimes found family life a little heavy. I felt the need for some breathing space, independence and a profound change in my day-to-day life. The key to this was provided by journeys beyond the boundaries of France, far away from the organized and burdensome framework of my bourgeois family life; wonderfully strenuous journeys that reinstated in me the quiet and calm that I lacked.

My first big trip was in 1952, when I was 17 years old, and I set out with a close friend on a cycling tour of England. Following exhaustive effort, we succeeded in persuading our parents and the school management that the objective of our trip — to improve our English language skills — was so lofty as to justify even a temporary hiatus in our schoolwork. Of course, we promised to return quickly in order to take the end-of-year exams. While they were still struggling with their doubts, we were already on the road.

The trip lasted about four months, from early June to the end of September. We covered between 200 and 250 kilometers per day, sleeping by the roadside in a small tent, an essential part of our luggage on this grueling journey. Our objective was to make it to a labor camp we had heard about while still in France. The camp, which housed the laborers from the nearby road works, was located on the England/ Scotland border and we hoped to work there in order to earn the money that we needed for the rest of our journey. We arrived at the camp only to discover that most of its inhabitants were Poles who had served in the Anders Army during World War II.[14] The work was not at all easy. The roads we laid crossed forests and the main tool at our disposal was a gigantic, very heavy hammer, with which we smashed stones and boulders. It was hard labor, but brought joy and even a spiritual uplift. My encounter with stubborn Mother Nature awakened in me energies that at last could be released. For the first time in my life, I felt that I had almost complete control over my strengths, both physical and emotional. I sang endlessly, I was happy; there was an almost animal feeling of victory and especially of liberation, of escaping from all the residues I had accumulated for so many years. In time, after five or six weeks of hard, boring, Sisyphean labor, I changed my mind slightly and lost some of my initial enthusiasm.

Shortly afterwards, we left the camp, my friend and I. The circumstances of our departure were unusual and not very pleasant: The Poles who lived in the camp made a habit of getting drunk on

---

14   Władysław Anders (August 11, 1892 –May 12, 1970) was a general in the Polish Army and later a politician with the Polish government-in-exile in London. In 1941, he established an army in the Soviet Union, comprised of Polish refugees. He led his troops toward the Middle East, where they fought alongside the British Army in World War II.

Saturday nights. They used to drink such huge quantities of alcohol as to be completely out of control. One Saturday night, an evil spirit entered them and at around midnight they decided to attack us young boys in the small hut in which we lived. They pounded violently on our door and when we realized that we were in a very bad situation, we decided then and there to get away. We jumped out of the back window, holding on tightly to our modest belongings, ran towards our bicycles and cycled for our lives. We didn't even wait for our previous week's wages that we were supposed to receive the following day. It was an extremely unpleasant experience, but we managed to get away unscathed. After that, we cycled for a few days until we reached London, and then we split up. He was a classmate and actually the best friend I had, but the hardships we had shared had gnawed away at the wall of our friendship and we decided that it was better to separate than to ruin our relationship.

My friend rode his bicycle back home and I stayed on in England for a further six weeks, returning home a few days before the start of the school year, which, at that time, began in early October. I found employment in Kent, where I worked mainly harvesting cherries. Once I'd saved enough for a ticket on the cross-channel ferry and to live on until I returned home, I set off once again on my bicycle. The ferry took me from New Haven to Dieppe in France and I cycled the rest of the journey home. A few kilometers before Paris, the handlebar on my bicycle broke and I was obliged to push it the rest of the way. In Paris, I slept in a public car park and when my money ran out, I made do with one baguette a day. Of course, I didn't have enough money to repair the bike or to buy a new one, but after about a week I found a truck that was heading for my hometown — some 500 kilometers from Paris — and I made it home safely. That was my first solo journey and involved a good deal of adventure. Being apart from my uncle, aunt and Annette had done us all good, but the joy when I returned home was genuine and I was moved by our reunion.

Still, throughout all those years I never really managed to feel part of the family. My uncle and aunt hoped I would feel like their son, but I resisted surrendering to my feelings and never allowed myself to relate to them as my real parents. To this day, I regret this wicked stubbornness of mine, which now seems nothing more than childish. I always made a point of addressing them as *vous* — the formal "you," which is used to show respect or to maintain a certain distance or formality with the person you are talking to, rather than the informal *tu* — the direct, intimate form you would use in addressing a friend or family member. It was an expression of my uncompromising stubbornness, which deeply hurt my aunt and uncle. But I could do no different. I refused to see them as my parents; I felt that if I surrendered, I would be betraying the memory of my dead parents. To their dying day, I did not change my attitude towards Aunt Hilda and Uncle Milek. Today, I regret that behavior, but I understand the boy and the youth that I was. It consoles me to know that they were aware of how deeply I loved them, that I was tied to their home and I hope they understood my feelings and that there was a line I was simply unable to cross.

Daily life proceeded like that of a typical family and I behaved like any other boy my age. I enjoyed going out and playing sport with my friends. I accepted the authority of my uncle, who was quite strict in spite of being a very pleasant person. It was clear to me that this was how things should be and I played by the rules, even though following house rules and demands did not come easily to me. Revolt was something that was deeply ingrained in my soul. Even later, in my adult life, I found it hard to accept authority, a fact that manifested itself often during my military service and at work. However hard I worked at overcoming this trait of mine, which often proved counterproductive, I did not always succeed and often had to pay a high price for it. Until the age of 11, I had lived in a framework that was not compatible with the needs of a boy. The feeling that I was all alone in the world perpetuated certain traits in my personality, and the difficulty in accepting authority was but one of them. However, this "difficulty" might have given me the strength to cope with life by myself and now, as a part of my new family, a warm and embracing family, I found myself in a framework in which adults were making all the decisions on my behalf. I found this very hard to accept, even though I understood that this was the way things were done in families — parents set the rules according to which their children are expected to behave. On the one hand, I tried to reconcile myself to these rules because I knew they were right and to my benefit, but deep inside, I rebelled against them.

In the years that followed my trip to England, I had an almost obsessive need for long journeys. I seem to have felt suffocated and in need of those periods of "airing" in order to return to myself. So, for the next three years, until I was 20, I spent the summer months travelling to various European countries. I was quite wild on those journeys — sleeping on park benches and in railway stations — and I was always short of money. I was probably driven by some adventurous urge in my personality and my close friends often warned me that these trips were destined to end badly. In modern terms, I was a backpacker and, as such, was a few decades ahead of my time. I made a point of being alone on those trips; the freedom to make my own decisions charged me with positive energy and made me happy.

When I was 18 years old, my uncle and aunt decided that the time had come for me to obtain French citizenship. They dealt with the formalities and, finally, I was awarded the status of a French national. From that moment, I was no longer required to report to the police at given times, as I had until then. I was also provided with an identity card and a French passport. I don't recall being particularly excited by being granted French citizenship, nor did it hold any special significance for me, but there is no doubt that Uncle Milek and Aunt Hilda were very pleased and considered it a great achievement.

Whether it was an inherent personality trait, or perhaps a natural response to what I had experienced in my childhood, for many years I was troubled by constant and relentless thoughts of revenge; numerous were these acts that I felt in my heart and planned in my mind, numerous were the thoughts that accompanied me during the years of my childhood and teens. Until one day, I don't remember exactly when, I stopped occupying myself with this matter and was sucked into a new reality. However, the urge for revenge remained rooted somewhere deep within me and since I probably never found the time to deal with it, it somehow continued to be present. The urge sprung from a deep hatred that I bore in my heart, but above all, I was troubled by the humiliation I had experienced and the memories of the painful sights I had seen all around me. The Germans had behaved toward the Jews as to inferior, despicable animals, as if we were no longer members of the human race. This insult was carved deep in my awareness and infuriated me.

In 1954, when I was 19 years old, I travelled to Brussels in order to "execute" a Jew who, according to Mr. Hourmont, was the man who had betrayed my parents. I was able to find the name of the neighborhood in which he had lived during the war and was determined to carry out my plan. I had decided to locate and interrogate him and if I was convinced that he was indeed involved in the arrest of my parents and other Jews, as I had been told, I would kill him. I told no one of my intentions, except for Annette, who was the same age as me, but she apparently didn't take my secret plan seriously. I suppose that an ordinary person who is deeply involved in the regular flow of life would not believe that in the heart of anyone else there could be so powerful an urge as to motivate him to carry out such an act of madness. I set off on my secret mission.

It was my first journey to Belgium since leaving for France in 1946. I had left Belgium as a boy, eight years earlier, with a disturbing past and an obscure future and returned as a young man who had not yet settled the scores of his childhood. It was also the first time, since we had separated at my aunt and uncle's home in France that I was reunited with Aunt Angele. It was the summer of 1954, a Sunday afternoon, the Christian day of rest. The streets of Brussels were empty and quiet. I boarded the same tram we had used to travel from the town center to our suburban neighborhood. The route had not changed; the streets were very familiar, it was as if time had stood still. I arrived at the final stop and disembarked from the tram. My return to the neighborhood was a jarring, almost surrealistic, experience. I froze on the spot. My feet stood on the same cobbled surface of the small town square on which my parents' feet had trodden 11 years earlier, when I accompanied them for the last time to the tram stop. Time had not dulled the pain, but it was a different kind of pain. It was no longer the same unbearable yearning I had felt when still in Belgium, or during my first years in France. It had been replaced by a rage at what had happened to my family;

a contained but powerful fury that required expression; a fury that grew stronger as I approached the day on which I might succeed in discovering the man who had betrayed my parents.

Nonetheless, I also felt a kind of relief. It was a feeling that increased as I drew closer to the neighborhood. As I approached the familiar streets, I was filled with joy, but also a kind of anxious excitement at the imminent meeting with Aunt Angele. I hadn't informed her of my arrival and I don't remember if we had corresponded. Later, when I tried to explain to myself the reason for the lack of communication between us for all those years since I had left for France, I could find none. It seemed we had both tried to bury our memories and to forget as much as possible the horrors of the past. I expect that Aunt Angele, with her gentleness and self-restraint, had feared that such a connection would have disrupted my current life.

I therefore didn't know that she had moved house. As I was marching toward the familiar house, suddenly I saw them. It had been the home of the elderly couple with the Pekinese dog. It was a corner house, surrounded by a larger garden than the one at her previous house. Although a large hedge surrounded the house, it was possible from a certain angle to see some of it from the street. As I said, it was a Sunday, the day on which families come together. Through the bushes, I saw the entire family sitting round a garden table — Aunt Angele, Uncle François, their son René and his wife Suzette — all those people I had been so close to as a child and with whom I had hoped to share my life.

I saw them all sitting there so relaxed, drinking coffee and talking quietly under the fruit trees that grew in the well-tended garden. I peeped in from the street and saw the four of them. There were also two or three other people with them in the garden, friends or relatives. I found it hard to take that difficult step towards them and to embrace them all. I stood for a few minutes and many pictures flashed in front of my eyes: scenes from the past that now appeared part of a world to which I no longer belonged. So much time had passed since then and my life had changed so much, and here, in front of me, Aunt Angele was sitting full of life, talking with everyone, laughing out loud, joking as she used to. A wave of emotion washed over me and I stopped for a moment to gather my wits. I thought I should overcome my excitement before taking a step forwards and joining that cheerful group.

All around there was the pleasant calm of the Sunday afternoon. The voices of children emanated from neighboring houses, a tranquil complacency permeated the air. Modest, lovingly tended gardens surrounded the houses, the flowers bloomed and a soft summer afternoon sun gave the scene a special kind of splendor. How things had changed since that troubled period during which I lived there. After waiting a few moments longer on the pavement opposite Aunt Angele's home, completely engrossed in reflections of the past, I decided to take one small but significant step further. Full of genuine happiness, I crossed the short distance that separated us and stood in front of them, like some ghost suddenly appearing from out of nowhere. Everyone seemed to freeze, as if unable to believe the natural apparition unfolding in front of them. Two or three of them asked me immediately, "Are you little Henri?" (the name by which they had known me) and when I said "yes," there was a giant explosion of emotion. They stood up as one and touched me, as if to check I was real. The laughter, the joy and the tears mingled together. With tears in her eyes, Aunt Angele came and hugged me tight and at that moment I knew that I would never again lose contact with this woman. And from that day until her death, she was, in every sense, a member of my closest family and I used to visit her from time to time in Brussels.

For almost two weeks I stayed with Aunt Angele and Uncle Francois, spending my days searching for the man who had betrayed my parents. I searched desperately for this needle in a haystack and, of course, I did not find him. No one knew when he had disappeared. Elderly people who had known him assumed he had been taken captive and might have perished, despite his desperate attempts to survive by betraying other Jews. My failure to find him weighed heavily on me. Here I was, finally, at the age and in the place at which I was supposed to realize my life's desire, and it wasn't happening. Thus, I was left full of this urge for revenge, to which there was now added the sharp frustration at not having found any release. I remember well my mental state when I left Brussels. As far as I was concerned, it had been a vital assignment, driven by an extremely powerful existential significance. For me, the assignment had donned a more universal aspect; I saw it as a mission. Hence, I felt a huge disappointment that I had let my parents down as well as all those other Jews on whose behalf I hoped to complete my undertaking.

At the age of 20, I left home to begin my university education in another city. Throughout my student days, I worked for my living even though my aunt and uncle would have been happy to finance my studies. On this matter, they had intended, in the most natural way possible, to exercise complete equality between Annette, who was also studying away from home, and me. But I wouldn't allow them to pay for me. It was an instinctive reaction on my part, an unequivocal desire not to be beholden, to achieve everything I could through my own efforts. I worked at different jobs, including the post of discipline counselor at a vocational school, a position often held by students. It was a good period in my life. I enjoyed my work and was gratified by the economic freedom it gave me. I was lord of my destiny, owing nothing to no one. During the vacations I went home and the reunions with Aunt Hilda, Uncle Milek and Annette were filled with warmth and joy.

At that time, I started to think about my position as a Jew. Although I was already a French citizen, with equal rights and independent of the establishment's generosity, I always knew that living in France was not my life's desire. I couldn't bear the duality of being both a French citizen and belonging to the Jewish community. At the same time, I started to take an interest in Zionism and discovered the writings of the founding fathers of the Zionist Movement. I read about Theodor Herzl and later read his book *The Jewish State*, followed by Leo Pinsker's *Auto-Emancipation* and more. I also read books that were less theoretical but with a direct affinity to settlement in Israel, like that of Yosef Baratz on the establishment of the first kibbutz, Degania Alef, and Arthur Koestler's experiences on a kibbutz, as well as others.

I visited Israel for the first time in 1956 and stayed for three months. I was overcome by a desire to see, to become familiar with and to get a sense of as much of the country as possible. I travelled throughout the land — visited the north, the south and Jerusalem; I stayed for a few days in Haifa, in the home of Uncle Avshalom, my mother's eldest brother, who had wanted to adopt me in 1946, and met his charming wife, Pnina. For the first time, I met my two cousins with whom I would have lived had my grandmother agreed that I move to Israel, a possibility which, as I have already said, she rejected out of hand.

For me, the greatest revelation on that first visit to Israel was the kibbutz. I spent two months on a kibbutz in the Negev and held numerous conversations with kibbutz members, some of whom impressed me deeply. Work on the kibbutz suited me and I felt wonderful. The Negev captured my heart. I was filled with feelings of primacy and a spirit of pioneering. For the first time in my life, I was naturally connected to my Jewish identity, which, in France, had felt forced or had required simulated declarations. I felt that everything I had experienced until then had been given a more urgent significance; in my eyes this had now become the only true purpose and the time had come for me to realize it.

Work in the fields, the feel of the land, the rifle sometimes hanging on my shoulder as I worked (after I had gained experience at a shooting range), the conversations with kibbutz members deep into the night, and the additional books I read all gave me the chance to follow my own path in life. No other lifestyle met so many of my needs at that time as did life on the kibbutz. Another point of interest was the mutual language I immediately found with those *kibbutzniks*. Some of them had been born in the country, while many others had come from a variety of places, some even before the establishment of the state, between 1946 and 1947; most of them had taken part in Israel's War of Independence. I was extremely fond of these people and it very soon transpired that I felt a greater closeness to them than I did to the members of my community in France.

My short stay in Israel and on the kibbutz utterly changed me. I informed the kibbutz members that I would be back shortly. Some of the members with whom I had become closest believed that I would return, but the majority laughed at me and said, "Let's wait and see." Many other youngsters who had fallen in love with the kibbutz way of life, which was different from anything they had known before, had made declarations such as mine. Experience had taught my kibbutz friends that in many cases these declarations were hollow and made on the spur of the moment, but had no foundation other than some simple spontaneous wish. However, I knew I would return and live there. My connection with the land had been made. It had been an immediate affinity, as strong and as deep as the number of years I had known myself. I felt that everything that had happened to me until then would receive significance only if I were to fulfill my new dream and immigrate to Israel.

I returned to France, resumed my studies and went back to work as before. I thought that I had returned a completely different person, but maybe I hadn't changed that much, since I bore within me a foundation that immediately connected me to Israel. I had found what I had gone to look for, without knowing that I would indeed find the answers to the questions that I had been asking myself endlessly over the years. So, at the end of the 1957 school year, I packed a few belongings and traveled back to Israel, to the kibbutz on which I had spent a short while in 1956. This time I stayed on the kibbutz for almost a year. Throughout my stay, I continued with my studies and the plan was to return to France before my exams in order not to miss the next school year. This was made possible thanks to the help of a few good friends who sent me regular shipments of the year's study material. I studied diligently for three or four hours every day after completing my work quota for the kibbutz. I worked in fields of cereal crops from the early hours of the morning until the afternoon and each passing day provided me with a profound experience. In my heart, I was already forming a decision as to my future, but at that stage, I told no one about it.

I decided that if I found the kibbutz lifestyle sufficiently satisfying, I would remain there and not return to France; if I didn't, then I would reconsider my future in Israel. I believed I had found what I was seeking with regard to the kind of life I was hoping for. To my uncle and aunt I explained that my decision to spend a year on the kibbutz before finally immigrating was meant to allow me to check from up close whether kibbutz life really was what I strove for. It was supposed to provide me with practical experience before "diving in at the deep end." In retrospect, I realized that this experience really had been necessary. It was a year of fulfillment — I had contributed something, whilst also remaining true to my plans and did not miss a year of my education. I was able to tell myself with satisfaction that during that year I had been lucky. And then the time came for me to give serious consideration to my future path in life.

Working the land and feeling such a close proximity to nature were indeed a successful part of my initiation into life in Israel, but as time went on I became increasingly convinced that life on a kibbutz did not suit me. This came from a combination of feelings and realizations that had formed slowly before ripening into a single, unequivocal decision — life on kibbutz was not for me. This realization stemmed from several elements, starting with the sense of an unrelenting pressure to conform, to which was added a total lack of seclusion and the unavoidable invasion of one's privacy; all these disturbed me very much. Then there was the undisputed law of the collective, the famous "members' meeting" that really upset me, because some of the decisions that were made there often had the power to change the lives of individuals or even of whole families and I could never come to terms with this.

On the kibbutz, I met some extraordinary, high-quality people who made a huge impression on me, although they accepted wholeheartedly the "rules of the movement."[15] I understood that it was not possible to be "half a *kibbutznik*" or a "provisory" kibbutz member; if you are a kibbutz member you have to accept the rules of the game, for better and for worse. Your attitude has to be uncompromising; otherwise there is no point to the kibbutz. Or so I felt. With all my regrets and feeling somewhat disappointed with myself, I came to the

---

15  Every kibbutz in Israel was established by a youth movement, such as Kibbutz Ha'arzi (founded by Hashomer Hatza'ir), Kibbutz Hame'uhad (founded by the United Kibbutz Movement), Hakibbutz Hadati (founded by Bnei Akiva), etc. There was considerable competition and often animosity among these movements and only in 1981 did they unite under the title United Kibbutz Movement (UKM) that has its headquarters in Tel Aviv.

conclusion that my place was not on a kibbutz. There was also another reason that for years I avoided pondering, even with myself, and it had something to do with living in an isolated and closed community. I recall the feeling that gripped me every time I drove a tractor close to the main road. Is this the feeling a prisoner gets when he comes up close to a prison fence or wall? I would be overwhelmed by a kind of inexplicable yearning for the big city, the noise, the people, for freedom, in every sense of the word. In those days, I would banish these ponderings angrily. I would suppress those feelings, but I have no doubt that they, too, had their effect. Although my decision to live in Israel remained firm, in the short term, all my plans changed and I decided to return to France for an additional two or three years in order to complete my studies and get myself better prepared for emigration.

From that moment, something changed in my basic sense of being. Although I returned to France, my heart was no longer there. My head and soul were still in Israel and I tried in every way possible to reinforce my Israeli identity. I sought social contact with Israelis staying in Paris and became very friendly with an Israeli medical student, who gave me private tutoring in Hebrew in exchange for which I taught him French. There was not an Israeli singer who performed in Paris that I didn't go to see, nor any event connected with Israel that I didn't attend. I saw myself as an Israeli who was living temporarily in France, but whose soul was in the homeland. I felt the need to do something for Israel and the only way I knew was through the Jewish community. I also registered with the Federation of Jewish Students in France and became quite active. But disappointment was not far behind. It very soon became apparent that the Federation dealt mainly with the matter of Jewish communities and not quite so much with Israel, except for the organization of trips there. After some time, during which I tried to change the group's inclinations, I encountered some difficulties and decided that there was no point to my continued activism within such an organization.

The following event in 1960 finally convinced me that I had to resign. At the time when there was a powerful wave of antisemitism in the community, several Jewish community buildings were daubed with hateful graffiti. Consequently, several members, myself included, tried to organize a class for a group of students to learn to physically defend the community buildings and, especially, its members. At first, about 50 students turned up and we started practicing judo. However, within just a few weeks, there remained only a few volunteers and the defense program was canceled. Some of my friends and I were angered by this decision and I understood, once and for all, that my place was not there. I resigned from the Federation of Jewish Students together with a few other activists who were disappointed by the weakness of the federation's leadership.

My wanderlust never left me for a moment. Equipped with a backpack and a few books, I set out on a new voyage of discovery. In 1960, I travelled to Africa for three months. I had always been interested in the African continent and was especially keen to visit Senegal, where Uncle Milek and Aunt Hilda had started their married life and Uncle Milek had been head veterinarian. All his life, Uncle Milek had yearned to return to Africa and he appeared to have infected me with his powerful attraction to this continent, which made this trip something of a search for my roots. I don't know why I didn't go in search of my roots in Auschwitz. But, I began my search in Senegal, where I arrived by ship from Marseilles in the south of France. During the crossing, I had become friendly with a man who held a very senior position in the Ministry of Education in Dakar, the Senegalese capital. I think he was either the general manager or his deputy, and I learned from our conversation that he was close to President Léopold Sédar Senghor.

I admired Senghor and had read many of his poetry collections: *Chants d'ombre* as well as *Hosties noires*; I also followed his interesting ideas on the Négritude movement.[16] My new friend invited me to visit him at the end of my journey in Dakar. I travelled all over Senegal by hitchhiking or taking local buses and visited remote jungle regions. I was surprised to find some older people who still remembered Uncle Milek from the time that they, themselves, had worked for the French

16   Négritude (lit. "Blackness") is a literary and ideological movement developed in France in the 1930s by francophone black intellectuals, writers and politicians. Its founders included Senegalese president Léopold Sédar Senghor and others.

Colonial authorities. I also visited Mali, crossing this wide country until I reached Timbuktu and finally, I toured the Republic of Upper Volta (renamed Burkina Faso) and was very moved by meetings with the local elders who had known Uncle Milek. They were no less moved than I. In two or three places, they organized "Tam Tam" evenings for me with drums that echoed loudly throughout the region, calling the villagers to come and dance and join in the happiness. I became very emotional at these spontaneous gestures.

One evening, deep in the Senegalese jungle, just as I was preparing to get into my sleeping bag under the night sky, as I had done many times before, a very charming French-speaking man stopped by and invited me to his village. I accepted his invitation and joined his wonderful family for a meal and then slept in their straw hut. The following morning, my host handed me an envelope addressed to the President of France, General Charles de Gaulle. It appeared that he had once served in the Senegalese division of the French Army and he wished to convey his respect to President de Gaulle. He asked me to present the letter to him. On my return to France, I sent the letter to the Élysée Palace, the official residence of President de Gaulle, together with an explanation of my own. I don't know to this day, if he ever read it.

When I arrived in Dakar, I contacted my friend at the Ministry of Education, who welcomed me warmly and a few days later arranged an audience for me with President Senghor. I sat with the president for almost an hour, during which time I recited to him one of his poems that I had learned by heart. We discussed literature and the movement for the restoration of African culture, of which he was one of the founders. The welcome I received from President Senghor was very warm and simple, with no airs or graces, and I understood that he was quite amused by me. The idea of spending almost an hour in the company of a young man like me, devoid of all official status, must have pleased him and provided him with a unique opportunity to sever himself for a moment from the burdens of his daily routine. I was in seventh heaven and was impressed that he, too, enjoyed this unusual meeting. Senghor was a well-known intellectual and the conversation with him left a strong impression on me. I returned to France happy and fulfilled. My trip to Africa had been the realization of an adventurous dream and it severed me for quite a long time from the world of action and reality. It was now time to realize the true dream.

Time flew by and I was very busy. Those years in Paris were fascinating and rich with cultural and social experiences and all the countless pleasures that Paris could provide an inquisitive young man with a powerful lust for life. But, even as I lived life to the full, I yearned for Israel. I discussed my plans for immigrating to Israel with Aunt Hilda and Uncle Milek. Neither of them was Zionistic in the least. In his youth, Milek had been a supporter of the Bund in Lvov. Their love for Israel was typical of Diaspora Jews, but, to be honest, they were not party to the Zionist enterprise. It was a love that was undefined and non-committal, tempered by some excitement and perhaps even a little pride, but apart from a very basic thrill, none of it really interested them. They were outside the circle of events in Israel and did nothing on its behalf, like many Jews in France. They noticed my fervor, but were unaware of the motives and background that stood behind my decision. Predictably and in the way of parents, they were not happy by my decision to "make *aliyah*," as it was called in France. They thought I was nurturing fantasies that would certainly pass in time; a kind of childhood illness that everyone goes through in one way or another.

By the time they realized that this was not a passing whim, but a resolve that would not be blocked and that they did not have the power to stop me, they showed no objection, but were only filled with sadness because I would be leaving their lives, in about the same way I had entered it — in a flash. They knew I was going to the unknown, which is something that is unbearable for any parent. They knew, too, that we would see very little of each other because in those days people didn't travel as much as they do now. The departure from them was not easy. My relationship with my aunt and uncle was as strong as that of a son to his parents. I loved them both very much. Sadly, I had already become accustomed to being separated from my loved ones and each separation reminded me of the previous one.

And then there arose another, unexpected, problem that upset the whole process. I hadn't served in the French Army and was very keen to serve in the Israel Defense Forces. I knew of the agreement between the two countries, according to which any young man who serves in the army of one country is exempt from service in the army of the other one. I believed naïvely that this agreement applied to me, too, but it soon became apparent that I did not fill the conditions of this mutuality for two reasons: I was not French-born and I had been granted a deferment from army service in order to continue my studies, so that I was obliged to do my military service in France. Any other option was tantamount to draft dodging.

To help me solve this issue, I enlisted some friends, including a close friend who was a legal expert, who tried to find a legitimate way to avert the enlistment, but all his efforts failed. I, therefore, immigrated to Israel with the knowledge that I would never be able to return to France. Indeed, shortly after my arrival in Israel, some policemen arrived at my uncle's home in France and declared me missing, which meant that the moment I set foot on French soil I would be arrested by the authorities. I was very uncomfortable with this situation; in spite of everything, France was dear to me. That country had taken me in and I had become a normal person there, due in large measure to the French education system, which gave me its best and even left its mark on my worldview. Moreover, I had left a family there as well as many friends and memories and places I was tied to. Would I really never see them again? The situation certainly weighed heavily on the way I felt. But in those days, nothing in the world could stand up to my determination.

# CHAPTER FOUR

## *A NEW PAGE AND MORE TO COME*

My immigration to Israel in 1961 signaled another new chapter in my life. My first meeting with the Israeli establishment is carved in my memory as a pleasant one. Shortly after my arrival in the country, I was summoned to the offices of the Jewish Agency at the port of Haifa, where, after filling in the necessary forms, I was sent to the customs clerk. My belongings consisted of a few dozen books, some articles of clothing, an alarm clock, a transistor radio and a guitar, which were all stuffed into a travel bag. The clerk scrutinized the bag with a look of wonder on his face. He said nothing, but pulled out an official customs form and asked me to fill out a declaration with a list of the duty-free goods that I wished to bring into the country as part of my new immigrant rights. I listed two objects that I'd have been happy to bring to Israel: my old bicycle and an ancient 1940s motorbike, on which I had crossed the length and breadth of France and Europe in the course of my many journeys. The clerk appeared shocked; he then attempted, very patiently, to explain to me my rights as a new immigrant to Israel and to persuade me to add to my list some additional items — essentials, according to him — that I would most likely need in the future. I told him I had no interest in doing so, since I was going to enlist in the military and would have no need for such stuff.

The charming clerk obviously got the gist of the person he was dealing with and, from that moment on, he took things into his own hands. Without asking for my opinion, he grabbed a pen and filled in the form with a long list of items, starting with a car, then adding electrical appliances, and ending with a dinner service plus anything else he could think of! When he had finished writing, he handed me the form and asked me to sign it, which I did, of course. The clerk added that I would be able to bring the goods into the country after I had completed my military service, so I had plenty of time to get myself organized. He was a delightful man and his genuine concern for my future made a deep impression on me. And indeed, I later brought some of the items from the list, including some domestic appliances that were absolutely essential, as I discovered later. That was my first encounter with the establishment in Israel and I came away from it feeling optimistic and brimming with hope.

Nonetheless, reality, at least initially, was not always easy. Once again, I found myself with the status of a "stranger in a new environment," a feeling that was very familiar to me, was highly charged and which had repeated itself several times in my life. I had immigrated to Israel through pure choice, but the joy and fulfillment that flooded through me did not prevent the omnipresent feelings of alienation and estrangement. The differences in mentality, culture and behavior reawakened certain experiences from the past, but the main obstacle of all was the language that seemed like an impassable barrier needing to be conquered and taken control of as quickly as possible. I resolved to achieve complete fluency in the Hebrew language; I decided to become an Israeli in every way. As I saw it, linguistic fluency and military service were the two most important elements in the integration process, and this was the order in which I planned things: First the language, then military service, and it was thus that I acted.

I studied at a kibbutz *ulpan*[17] where half the day was spent working on the kibbutz and the other half was devoted to language study. My classmates were young, new arrivals from various countries

17   An *ulpan* is an institute or school for the intensive study of Hebrew.

around the world, each with his or her reason for emigrating. However, the atmosphere in the *ulpan* was not serious enough for me. The evenings were inevitably devoted to parties and dancing and my fellow students were drawn to every available temptation in an atmosphere of complete liberty, frivolity and utter detachment from the reality outside the *ulpan* and kibbutz. They seemed to have forgotten the reason for which they were there. I might have been a little too tough with myself, but I was quite determined to make full use of those months prior to my army enlistment. I spent my evenings studying in my room, absolutely detached from the lively bustle surrounding me. After a month and a half on the kibbutz *ulpan*, I decided to leave and to move to a city *ulpan* in Haifa, where the studies were more intensive. The kibbutz *ulpan* principal and my teacher opposed my decision in every way possible.

They begged me to stay and to complete the study program there, warning me that my decision would ruin my future. However, when all their efforts at persuasion failed, they decided to take action: They locked all my belongings in the kibbutz storeroom. Their concern was touching, but I did not surrender and with the help of various forms of subterfuge, I managed to release my possessions and moved to a regular day *ulpan*, where I studied for a brief period and then left the rest of my language learning to the army — the best place in my eyes to learn colloquial Hebrew. A few months later, I met the woman who would become my wife. She, too, was serving in the army and she made an important contribution to my long and arduous road toward turning the Hebrew language into a part of who I would become.

The study of a new language as a means of communication is a complex process, fraught with pitfalls and a lot of frustration and it requires a fair amount of daring. At its foundation, there is a measure of alienation that gradually dissolves as integration into society becomes more natural. The study of a new language loads one's memory with a large number of new words, which have to be absorbed in countless ways and, after some hesitation and exhaustive effort, a word matures and formulates into a sentence. All too often, there is the problem of the wrong or anachronistic use of words; for example, when the word is the right one but unsuitable to the circumstances; sometimes it's too literary, too highbrow, too lowbrow, or no longer in fashion.

For instance, I once pointed out to my girlfriend that she was "fishing in murky waters." The loud burst of laughter that resulted made it obvious that I had made a mistake. She drew my attention to the fact that not every word in the dictionary is suitable in day-to-day usage.

So, sometimes, I conducted linguistic experiments on the people I was talking to, by integrating a new expression into a sentence I had composed and, from the response, I knew if the expression had been appropriate. Responses were varied. There were some who corrected me and I was grateful to them; others smiled strangely and I realized that I had made a blunder; and there were others, who were too polite or too shy and lacked the nerve to point out my error; or by not wanting to embarrass me, they let me continue with my mistake. Actually, this was the greatest hardship. In the beginning, at least, being a new immigrant has a derogatory effect on one's self-confidence, since when you say something funny or that makes people smile, you feel terrible. A new immigrant, who, in his country of origin had belonged to the educated classes, can suddenly feel ignorant and stupid. I experienced several slipups that to this day cause me to cringe at the memory. Nevertheless, I decided not to seek sanctuary among other French speakers, which could have been a simple solution and one that many new immigrants choose. I gritted my teeth and moved on.

Yet, language was not my only difficulty; the lack of a Jewish education also bothered me considerably. I befriended people who had had a similar formal education to my own, but my knowledge in the most basic Jewish and Israeli subjects was not even equal to that of a local ten-year-old. Since I made a point of making friends only with Israelis, I often found myself excluded from a conversation, especially when it dealt with references from Hebrew literature, the Bible or ancient history. I was in a hurry to make up for all these discrepancies and felt that by doing so I would achieve the "Israeli" status that I longed for.

And there was another thing: The behavior of Israelis was different from what I had been used to, even from what I had known during my stay on the kibbutz. When a debate breaks out at social evenings, everyone has his or her say and when the arguments turn lively and challenging, they raise their voices and no one listens to what is being said as each one is too busy making his or her own point. In France, people are not so vehement in voicing their opinions and proving their point. They tend to give in politely, wait for things to wind down and only then do they utter what they had intended to say. It's a relaxed dynamic of communication in which there is real interest in what the other has to say. Here, on the other hand, when I waited patiently for my turn to say my piece, it was already too late; everyone else had already clarified the issue under debate and moved on to another subject. I said nothing and remained frustrated. Nor did the raised voices in the course of a conversation do anything to encourage me to participate and I often chose not to respond.

The differences in mentality and other unfamiliar things made my social integration in Israel significantly more difficult and awakened in me some unpleasant memories of various other periods in my life in which I was forced to struggle for my position in society. Of course, there was no room for comparison. In Israel, the most you can talk about is some unpleasantness, the kind that usually passes, or at least fades away gradually. I accepted this as part of the package known as "*aliyah*." With the passage of time, I found my way and my style with which to express myself and I flowed with the new reality I had chosen to live in and became a part of it.

I enlisted in the Israel Defense Forces (IDF), which, as far as I was concerned, was one big mystery. I felt I was being led through some automatic system without knowing where I was going. After basic training I was offered an officer's commission and, because I was a university graduate and 26 years old, I wasn't required to take the officer's training course. However, I didn't agree to this arrangement and asked to follow the usual route. I had been used to much personal freedom in the vibrant city of Paris. Now, an interesting revolution was taking place in my new army life and, in order to cope with it, I had to use a considerable amount of humor. I also suddenly found myself in the company of eighteen-year-olds with whom I shared day-to-day hardships that were new and foreign to us all. Despite the obvious differences in education among us, I was adamant about doing the full quota of military service.

The thing that most troubled me on a day-to-day level was the language barrier. Carrying out orders that are fired at you with the speed of a machine gun, when you don't always understand what's being said, and so you try desperately to copy what the others are doing, is not something to be taken for granted. The youngsters and the officers around me were considerate and they tried to a certain extent to help me tackle the challenge; now and then I was even assisted by people who could translate into English.

Above all, I missed having a private corner of my own, where I could place a few personal possessions and, especially, to take some time out whenever possible. This need intensified under military conditions, when you are never alone for a moment. My personal belongings were stored in the homes of friends and family in various parts of the country, where I also spent my short vacations from the army. I spent many Sabbaths on base and ever since then I have hated cholent, the traditional Sabbath stew cooked overnight on a very low heat and was served to the soldiers who didn't go home for the weekend. The army cholent was served cold and its vapid taste remained in my mouth for many years. However, I also spent many vacations at the home of Uncle Avshalom and Aunt Pnina, who took excellent care of me.

My official status in the IDF was that of "lone soldier." But to me, all the hardships and discomforts were no more than a matter of inconvenience that were negated by the very fact of my doing military service, which was a huge source of satisfaction. Military service gave me the opportunity to be drawn full speed into the Israeli experience and in the most significant manner. I have no doubt at all that it was in the IDF that I became an Israeli. All of a sudden, I was exposed to a human reality that was at once rich and problematic, under circumstances that were not always comfortable or fundamentally equitable, during the first few months at least. My participation in the IDF provided me with a comfortable field of observation that was as broad as it was deep. The unique conditions, the strict regime and the obligatory interdependence all turned me into an inseparable part of this whole, without giving a thought to the process as it was taking place. I was released from the army with the feeling that I was better prepared for the future that awaited me. Looking back, the decision to do military service in order to gain an entry ticket to life in Israel was the right one.

I am not a "one of the lads" type. Unlike in Europe, this kind of group companionship is common in Israel and I am apparently unsuited to this sort of relationship; in this respect I have remained somewhat different. However, as in the past, when it was necessary, I reactivated the adaptation mechanism within me that enabled my integration into the society around me until I felt a real part of it. My ever-closer relationship with my Israeli girlfriend, Yehudit, also helped the process. Not only did I improve my Hebrew thanks to her, but I also got to know her friends, with whom I soon found a common language.

About two or three years after my emigration I was contacted by representatives of the French Consulate in Israel, who tried to persuade me to return to France in order to complete a year of compulsory military service. I told them I was unable to do so because I had already served in Israel. I pointed out that I was getting older and had to start considering my future, my employment and the course that my life was to take in the new country I had chosen to live in. For some reason, the consular staff appeared sympathetic to my circumstances. I had the impression that they felt awkward making this demand, but they were obliged to follow orders. As for me, I have already pointed out that I felt uncomfortable with the situation. Ultimately, it had been France that had given me an identity and an education; it had also given me strength and some sense of belonging. My life there had been pleasant and good and I had a feeling that I was betraying France; I felt guilty for not having fulfilled the miniscule debt with which I should have repaid France and that the way I had left was dishonorable. This feeling stayed with me for quite a while until I concluded that I had done the right thing and that you can't please everybody.

One day in 1966, the telephone rang at home. The secretary of the French Consulate in Tel Aviv was calling to inform me that President de Gaulle had granted a pardon to "criminals" of my ilk and that I had been officially pardoned. The secretary concluded by jokingly informing me that I was free to visit France with no fear of arrest. I felt relieved and very moved. The only stain on my whole immigration process had now been erased. I knew, too, how important this was to my family in France and I quickly sent them the good news. Now I could visit the scenes of my youth and the home in which I had known such happy times, and I could once again meet the friends and acquaintances whom I had loved. In the years since emigrating I must have buried this matter deep within my heart. I liked the idea that I was now able to visit France one day. Another circle had closed.

Yehudit and I got married in February 1964 at the Tel Aviv Rabbinate. It was a brief and modest ceremony that lasted less than one hour. Even before our guests had had time to put on their coats, the staff had prepared the small hall for the next couple. To the mortification of the bride's parents we didn't have the money for a more extravagant wedding, and neither did they. But, as far as we were concerned, it was of no importance. My uncle and aunt from France, Hilda and Milek, did not attend the ceremony. They wanted very much to be there but I advised them to postpone the trip until the summer, when they could spend more time with us. My Uncle Avshalom from Haifa led me to the *chuppah* (wedding canopy). Avshalom, his wife, Pnina, and their son and daughter-in-law represented my family at our wedding. The past, especially the distant past, often reappears in full force at such crossroads of one's life and, for me, as the ceremony began, I pondered over what awaited me. Suddenly, there appeared the connection between me — the bridegroom about to take the most important step of his life — and the boy who was still hiding deep within me. And at that moment I thought of my parents. In my imagination I saw them partaking in the wedding ceremony. They flashed by and disappeared and, of course, no one was aware of what was happening inside me, but it was a powerful moment that became deeply etched.

The same thing happened at the wedding of our daughter. Some of our friends claimed after the ceremony to have seen tears in my eyes. As I stood beside my daughter under the *chuppah* I must have been unable to hide my emotions. For a split second, a connection was formed between my fate and me. I had been alone in the world; a lonely boy who knew nothing about his family, and here I now was in Israel, surrounded by friends, at my daughter's wedding. I didn't shed a tear as some people had surmised; I was simply unable to hide the storm and control the complicated emotions. But, as we stood under the *chuppah* at my son's wedding, I was aware once again of that unique feeling, a kind of transcendental moment that reconnected me with my fate and again I was flooded with the same feeling that was so hard to quell. However, this time, no one noticed the storm raging in my heart, because I was aware of it and had learned to control the situation. I am incapable of considering such an event in a normal way. Each occasion reaches proportions that are almost ethereal.

What can be more normal than when a baby is born to your children? However, every time it has happened, I see it as a recurring miracle that was repeated with the birth of each of my grandchildren. Can this all have happened to me, whose childhood passed by on life's periphery? I sometimes find it hard to believe, so many years later, that I, too, am a grandfather, like everybody else. You need a strong personality and emotional powers if you are to avoid being carried away by the surge of emotions that well up and overflow. Although, in the course of my life, time has not even slightly managed to contain my powerful emotions, my self-control has improved.

In my day-to-day life, the future came knocking at my door and life pulled me along. Like many others my age, I moved forward both professionally and personally. I was drawn into the reality of Israel with two clear objectives: To devote myself to work and contribute what I could to the country that had welcomed me into its bosom and was kind to me; and to take care of and enjoy my family. Quite naturally, the past has lived on in me and I now have a healthy relationship with it. It doesn't disturb me. I have no discourse with it. I have never turned to it as the present has always been enough for me. Many of my friends knew nothing of my distant past; others knew that I had had an unusual childhood, but were unaware of the details; while others knew that I had been orphaned at an early age, but we never discussed the issue. When we were young, it all seemed perfectly natural to me and later, as adults involved in the reality of our lives, the majority did not talk about their past. But a few who had been involved in the establishment of the state or had served in the Palmach[18] or the Irgun[19] told stories that contained a powerful aroma of times gone by. I felt no need to tell the story of my own past, which was devoid of all luster and, above all, I wanted to avoid arousing pity or condolence.

There was a burning need inside me to act on behalf of Israel, which was fulfilled by my employment in the civil service, shortly after my release from the army. I spent most of my adult life working in the service and I felt that my rich life experience was often a great help in carrying out sensitive missions abroad. The intensity of life within a unique society and the challenge-filled activity demanded absolute commitment. Most of my colleagues were native Israelis and they welcomed me with open arms. Moreover, I often felt that my presence among these people, most of whom had grown up in the country and had a background so different from my own, aroused in them a curiosity and willingness to learn about my world and to include me in their own. I envied them at first for having deep roots in the country and for their sense of belonging that they seemed to take for granted. It was so different from me, for whom the feeling of alienation and being a new arrival was an inseparable part of my makeup. But these differences did not create distance. On the contrary, they aroused mutual interest and, after a short time, I had a true sense of belonging among the people and in the workplace.

I became fully integrated into the group of people among whom I worked, although there still remained some of the natural distance of an outside observer as I found it important to preserve who I was. Strangely enough, years later, one of my colleagues confided that he had envied me specifically for this "dissimilarity" of mine. He saw in me a man of the world, with European manners and social graces, traits that often turned out to be very useful in the course of my

---

18    The Palmach (Hebrew acronym for "striking forces") was the elite fighting force of the Haganah underground movement in the Yishuv (Jewish community) during the British Mandate for Palestine.

19    The Irgun (Hebrew acronym for National Military Organization) was a right-wing Zionist paramilitary organization that operated in British Mandate Palestine between 1931 and 1948.

work. I found it a great honor to belong to this group of people, who enabled me to be party to ideas and actions that were vital to the state. I was part of a unique family that grows and develops under special conditions in which it does what is expected with enthusiasm and a sense of accomplishment. I could dream of nothing more.

I occasionally go back to meet and confront my past, which is like a shadow — always there, sometimes hiding, sometimes revealing itself in various shapes, depending on the aspect of its exposure. I was on a visit to Belgium with my wife, many years after I had immigrated to Israel, when Aunt Angele announced that a surprise awaited me. She told me that someone there wanted to meet me. Without much ado, she led us to the home of an elderly couple who lived a short distance from her. The home to which we were taken was pretty and unpretentious, an old-fashioned Belgian-style house with furniture that was rather heavy but pleasing to look at and according a homey atmosphere. The couple was very pleased to meet us and welcomed us warmly into their living room, which was quite dark but had a feeling of calm to it. Our host was sitting in a deep armchair, which was upholstered in a dark, handsome fabric; he stood up as soon as he saw us, shook our hands enthusiastically and returned to his chair. A blanket covered his knees and we realized that he had some trouble walking. He had been the principal of the school I had attended as a boy.

I recognized the principal, although I would not have done so had I met him in the street. His full image returned to me in all its glory in the split second it took me to inspect him and I was able, immediately, to tie him to the image of the man I remembered from my childhood: young, energetic and always distinguished. In school, he had reflected authority, due to his personality and aristocratic mien. No pupil ever dared undermine him, especially when he occasionally appeared in the schoolyard during recess to ensure that everything was alright. If his glance happened to fall on a specific child, that child would stop in his tracks and appear confused. He had also had the respect of his teaching staff, as was obvious by their behavior when they were in his presence. He was always impeccably dressed, polite, refined and determined. I never heard him raise his voice.

His excitement at meeting us was obvious. He gave me a long look and smiled, "Well, and how is Monsieur Dieudonné?" And again, there was his charming smile, the same piercing look that left one totally exposed; as he went on in his soft voice, "How can I ever forget that skinny boy, as nimble as a cat? Even now, I still see him with that suspicious look in his eyes, probing and forceful, following everything in his vicinity — an ever-present, vaguely obsessive awareness. Your glance went with me for many years. How can I forget?" And he added, "You have changed very much. From a restless boy, you seem to have grown into a relatively relaxed man, yet your glance does take me back quite a few years. I am so happy to see you again."

There was so much strength and so much love in this man. I watched him at length, wanting to say something, but the words were trapped, refusing to burst forth. Our eyes met, he smiled at me and I returned him a wan, shy, somewhat embarrassed smile. For a few moments, I returned to being that frightened boy, accepting the authority of this man who represented to me all the good and the enlightenment that I sought during the war. "Did you know at the time who I was and that I was living under a false identity?" I asked him. Again, he gave me an inscrutable smile, full of meaning, as if trying to hint at something I didn't know, something that remained locked in his brain and his heart, and no one could crack the secrets hidden behind that eminent expression on his face. My curiosity increased. The two women continued to converse, while between him and me there evolved a kind of relationship of which silence was a part. "I am beginning to believe that your role in the whole issue of my rescue was much greater than I had assumed. Can you tell me something I didn't know until now?" The man started to talk and I was enthralled. The enormous respect I had once had for him returned and enveloped me. I was being exposed to something amazing and to information that I had never known before. I wondered if Aunt Angele had known what I was about to hear, but never told me.

I learned that my old school principal had been active in the Belgian underground and he had known when I arrived at his school exactly who I was. He had worked hard on getting me integrated into school society, sparing no effort in explaining and excusing my frequent absences to the other teachers, who, of course, had not been in on the secret. In addition, I learned that there had been two other Jewish boys in my class; meaning there had been three Jewish kids in the class and none of us had known about the existence of the others. He was the only one who had known our secret and tried tirelessly to "put out fires" and to protect us. In fact, he had acted on behalf of the underground, which had had an operation for rescuing Jewish children. This man had displayed superhuman courage, putting his life in danger every single hour of every single day. It was obvious that, as he looked at me with his gentle smile, reflecting both happiness and sorrow, his brain was awash with thousands of memories. But he tried to keep his feelings under control, as would any other true hero.

This meeting, which took place about 25 years after World War II, reawakened in me harsh, as well as pleasant, memories that had mixed together and were stamped deep inside my heart. When we returned to Aunt Angele's home and mulled over the unique event we had just experienced, Aunt Angele turned to me and, with her characteristic directness, asked me, "Are you a good Jew?" She wanted to know if I practiced the religion and followed its demands. I was rather embarrassed and nodded my head as if to say, "So, so." Aunt Angele gave me one of her piercing authoritative looks and said, "What shall I tell your parents when I meet them in the next world?" and added with a ponderous note, "You should give this a lot of thought." Throughout the time I had stayed in her home as a child, she had never preached to me in so direct a manner. I wanted to hug her for what she said and for what she represented — a pure soul with a superior personality — but the relationship that had developed between us prevented me from doing so. As in the old days, we both practiced restraint.

A few years ago, my wife and I visited Malines (in Flemish, Mechelen) for the first time. It was from there that my loved ones had been transported to Auschwitz. We visited the town's small Jewish museum, built on the site of the transit camp from where

Jews were transported by train to be annihilated. During the visit to the museum, I saw photographs of General Falkenhausen,[20] the supreme commander of the German forces in Belgium; General Eggert Reeder, chief administrative officer of the occupying powers; and Major Philip Schmidt, commander of the Malines transit camp. Afterwards, I stood alone in the camp's huge courtyard into which the prisoners had been brought before being transported in the death trains. It's a large oblong-shaped space located in a suburb of Malines. The central courtyard is surrounded on all sides by residential buildings and it has a single high and wide entrance. The place served originally as barracks for the Belgian Army and later, during the war, it was reassigned as a transit camp under the management of the Germans. The buildings have since been renovated and new ones added and used as living quarters; but, in the middle, there remains the huge courtyard in which the Jews were held after their arrest. It was from there that my parents and aunt and uncle set out on their final journey. Having no control over my emotions, I was seeing the place in front of me, closed and fenced in with barbed wire, with threatening sentries and thousands of terrified people. My heart lurched and my senses became blurred. All around there was silence and the buildings appeared deserted. For a few moments, I felt myself trying to return to 1943 — the year my parents were brought there.

There is an archive above the Jewish museum in which secretaries and researchers are involved in documenting the details of all the inmates who spent time in the Malines camp during the war. One of the researchers received us politely and showed us the

20   Alexander von Falkenhausen was the chief military commander of the German occupying forces in Belgium and northern France. He headed the military administration of Belgium, while the civil affairs remained in the hands of the Belgian General Secretaries, who headed the ministries and dealt with the civil administration of the country as representatives of the government in exile in London. Belgium differed from the Netherlands, where both the military and civil administrations were managed by the Germans. It differed also from France where the civil affairs remained in French hands but were oriented to benefit from direct collaboration with the Germans.

camp's transport logbook with details on my Aunt Hanna'le, Uncle Salo and my parents. Next to my mother's name there was even a handwritten correction dated 1943, saying that Sara was the wife of Elias. In another list, dated 1942, I saw the names of Hanna'le and Salo. There were also documents detailing my parents' accommodation prior to their arrest. All the details in the documents were correct; and I am even mentioned by name and with correct details. The Germans had known of my existence but had clearly been unable to locate me.

After our visit to Malines, we went to the neighborhood in Brussels where I had lived with Aunt Angele. I showed my wife the place where I had last seen my parents as well as the church in which I had prayed. The church had been converted into a gym and a much larger church had been built next to the old one. We managed to locate the resident priest in the new church, an elderly man in his seventies. He told us that he had been very familiar with "my" priest, who had died several years earlier. He even told us what had become of him and described what he looked like. The descriptions matched my own memory of the priest I had known — a good and modest man, but not a man of stature; not like my school principal, who had been a member of the underground and had risked his own life in order to rescue Jewish children. The priest had not, it seemed, been cut from the same cloth and had continued to oversee his church congregation as if nothing of the war was happening around him.

With all the anomalies that characterized my childhood years, it could be said that I was also quite fortunate. Indeed, my luck can be summed up in one word — love. Love is the key to everything. It was and remains the source of my strength and my stamina. Most of the time, I was surrounded by people who loved me and I never felt any lack of love. I have always been with people who cared for me, who were guided by their concern for my security and my upbringing — my parents of course, Hanna'le and Salo and, later, Aunt Angele, Hilda and Milek. Even my immigration to Israel and integration into Israeli society were always backed by a great deal of acceptance and openness.

* * *

I am sitting on a train, on my way to a meeting in a small town in the south of Germany, which I have already visited many times in the past. Meticulously dressed in a smart suit and colorful tie, I am preparing for the meeting according to my habit — going over all the relevant facts, right down to the smallest minutia, and examining potential situations that might develop in the course of the meeting and as a result of it. As usual at this stage of my work, so close to a meeting, I have a general sense of relief. Not, heaven forbid, complacency, which could be catastrophic for a person like me, who often has to walk a tightrope. I try to be alert and focused, but beneath the cold and calculated persona, there lurks fervor and a sense of mission. I never lose sight of why I am here; all my resources are geared towards the meeting that will take place shortly. As I ponder, I glance at my fellow passengers, two women and three men. The three men opposite me are middle aged and engrossed in a lively conversation. The walls of the carriage are covered in a dark, soft and warm velvet fabric; the upholstery of my seat is pleasant and comfortable. Outside, the scenery is exquisite and the day's last sunrays penetrate the carriage through the windowpane. I sit back in my seat, a pleasant weariness spreads through my limbs, and my head is a little heavy, my senses dull.

> *I scrutinize the three men sitting opposite me. What I see are three German officers, the ones I saw in the photographs in the Malines Jewish Museum: General Falkenhausen, General Reeder and Major Schmidt. They are studying me, a mocking smile spreading over each of their faces. The train races through a tunnel whose walls block out the light in the carriage. The black space inside is suffocating and cuts my breath. I am gripped with terror, feeling paralyzed as the train reaches supersonic speed. I move my hand towards the revolver in my coat pocket and try to shoot them, but my body seems frozen, my right hand refuses to obey me; I try to rise, but my legs won't bear me. The three officers continue to pin their mocking eyes on me. And then, suddenly, something is released. My*

*body appears to surrender to my powerful will, my hand comes alive and three bullets slice through the air; the three Germans collapse in their seats. The presence of those three German soldiers had been troubling me on several other occasions since the visit to the Malines museum, but this time, it seems their fate has been sealed.*

I shake off the remains of the dream and stretch out my limbs, feeling more peaceful and relaxed than I have felt in a long time. A gentle smile spreads over my face. In the cozy and indulgent German train carriage the same five people still sit around me — next to me are the two ladies and opposite me sit the three men, still deep in conversation, as if absolutely nothing had happened. They were the three German officers I had just shot to death in my dream. I straighten up in my seat, ready to alight at my destination. The train halts, I climb down. It is late afternoon, thousands of people are milling about in a hurry, each in his own direction. I wander through the streets that have become so familiar to me from previous visits. I feel wonderful, absolutely alert and focused on what is about to happen. In a little while, I'll be attending the meeting I had so carefully prepared for and by this time tomorrow, I shall be home. I am always excited to land in Israel, where an action-packed week awaits me, with family, my friends in the choir and Verdi's opera *La Forza del Destino* — one of my favorites. It's a good routine that is pleasant to return to.

# EPILOGUE

This is not an autobiography. It is a kind of biography of my war; a war that did not come to an end in the summer of 1945, but remained a fixed pattern, the basis for everything that happened to me. It is the axis around which everything that happened subsequently moved — all the choices and all the decisions I made. Much of my activity in France was the aftereffect of the war and my emigration to Israel was its inevitable result. In itself, my emigration is of no interest. Millions of Jews immigrated to Israel during those years, but, for me, it was another round in my childhood experiences. Because of the burden I carry with me everywhere I go, most of the things I did or that happened to me involved larger struggles. Still, the resilience I built up during my childhood was of great help in overcoming my hardships faster and probably better than many others who had similar experiences.

My story is that of an ordinary boy who was suddenly sucked into a whirlwind of events over which he had no control and tried with all his might to somehow float and to survive. After the wave washed away part of his life, he continued to live as if he were an ordinary boy who had not experienced these harsh things. He lived his life as if nothing had happened. Although the burden of the past has remained a part of me, it has stayed solely my own. In the midst of that entire inferno there were even a few special moments. The God to whom I prayed in the small church in Belgium was very close to me. I am not sure that I believed for a moment that He would save me; I was never full of faith. But I felt a fondness for Him. He was friendly. I could see Him in pictures or crucified on the wooden cross that hung in the church. He had a presence. I could touch Him. I was careful to fulfill most of the demands of the Christian religion and the fact is that I was saved, which is why it was so hard for me to be separated from Him. I yearned to be a Christian by right, to be baptized and to continue in the Christian tradition that advocates good deeds for humankind. Deep in my heart I dreamed of being a missionary in Africa.

Nevertheless, my life took a different turn and I was obliged to say goodbye to my noble intentions. I felt alone when I arrived in France, because I didn't find a God who would be close to me. And when I refer to God, I refer also to all the elaborate rituals that go with religion. Perhaps, it was for this that I yearned — the atmosphere of the church, the colorful clothes worn by the priest, the shiny robes that I wore during prayers, the angelic songs of the choirboys, of whom I was one, the scent of incense and the taste of communion wafers.

At the beginning of my life in France I missed the church acutely, but gradually the yearning ceased to disturb my rest, and it eventually disappeared entirely from my life. I don't remember if I ever told my dear ones that I had sung in the church choir; nor do I know how my father would have accepted this. My mother, who was a free and liberal woman and loved music, especially opera, would certainly have understood and accepted the fact. But I had much to tell about my new life in France, which included a few hardships, but much stability and, above all, the love of my aunt and uncle towards me, to which, in time, I also opened my heart.

So, why am I writing this now? Why did I suddenly feel the need to reveal this chapter in my life? There is no unequivocal answer and all the answers have been known for a long time. Much has been written about that period of time, but it was important to me to understand how an eight- or nine-year-old boy managed to cope, virtually on his own, with those events without the protective outer layer of his family and home environment. I also wanted to understand the effect these events had on the rest of my life and I could do this only by telling the story, the reconstruction of which took quite a long time. Some of the events had been forgotten and some were hidden, locked securely in the dungeons of my memory. Most difficult of all was the decision to go back and open this "black box." Surprisingly enough, however, the moment the lock was broken, the memories resurrected themselves and more. The senses, the scents and the touch were all waiting quietly and patiently for my arrival.

For many years I had turned my back on my distant past, as if I wished to ignore its existence and yet, just a few years ago I started to ponder on it and found myself delving ever deeper into the details and the minutiae. Then, not yet satisfied, I began to search for information in documents and archives and the facts began to flow towards me in surprising quantities and scope from institutions involved in Holocaust research and the rescue of Jewish children in Belgium. With the help of all these factors, I was able to reconstruct parts of the events I had experienced in my childhood. The documents verified some of the facts that had, until then, not been completely clear to me and which provided me with some kind of additional substance to my memories, but no more than that.

Now that I have completed the task of writing my story, it seems as if my memory mechanism is deceiving me. Before writing my memoirs, all the various events had maintained a measure of sharpness. I had always felt they were a part of me, that they were within arm's reach and belonged to my very being. But the moment I connected to them, blew away the years of dust, exposed them to daylight, redesigned and dressed them in words, it was as if they were removed from my control — they were no longer the same events I had experienced up to now. The fine threads that connected me to them started unraveling, slipping out of my grasp and severing themselves from me; they are no longer mine, it is as if they belong to someone else. The feeling of closeness that allowed me to save them in all their vitality gradually disintegrated. Now those same events come back to me from beyond the written text and only thus am I able to experience them anew. Has something of their authenticity been lost on the way to the written word? Perhaps it was unavoidable. At long last, Nathaniel and my tin soldier in his cardboard box, who emerged out of the darkness one fine day, have found their rightful place.

One morning a few months ago, I opened my email inbox as usual and found a letter from the archive in Malines. I opened it and on the screen appeared four photographs one after the other: my father, my mother, Hanna'le and Salo. They filled the screen from edge to edge, looking exactly as I remembered them from our last meetings. I had never seen these photographs and certainly not in such a large size. These are most likely their final pictures. I have no idea under what circumstances they were taken, whether in a police cell in Belgium or earlier. In the photographs they are dressed in understated elegance — my father and Salo in jacket and tie, my mother and Hanna'le wearing coats. The pictures were taken in winter. My father appears quite tired; my mother looks sad, a look of distant desperation in her eyes; Hanna'le looks frightened, her beauty withered. As for Salo, even under such circumstances he maintains a proud, gentlemanly profile. It is strange how things come back to me, how they spring up before me at this particular time in my life, suddenly appearing on the computer screen, as if knowing that I am waiting for them here, now.

My father Elias

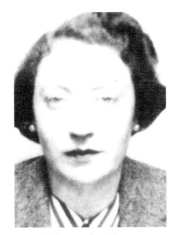

My mother Sara

Uncle Salo

Aunt Hanna'le